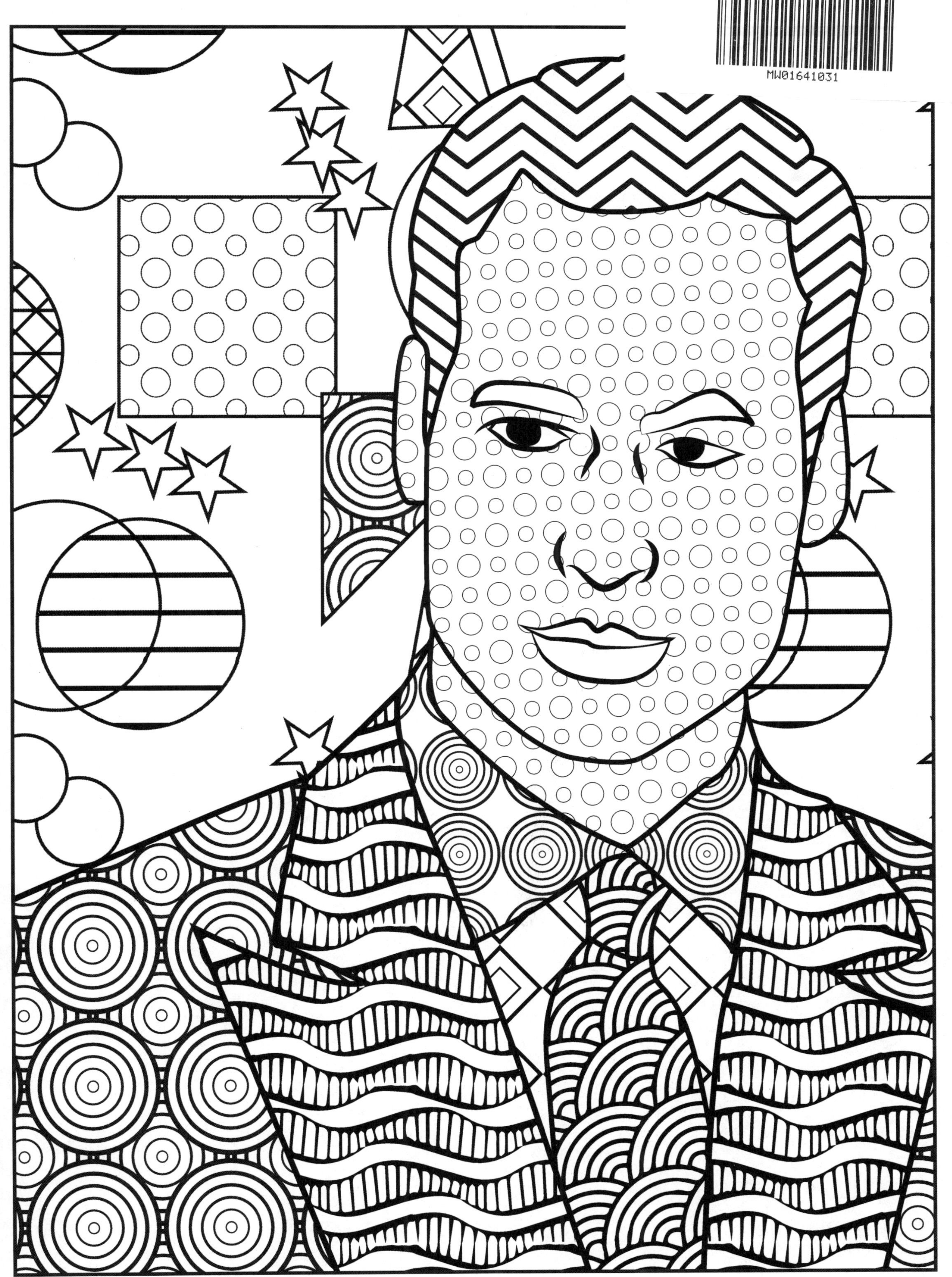

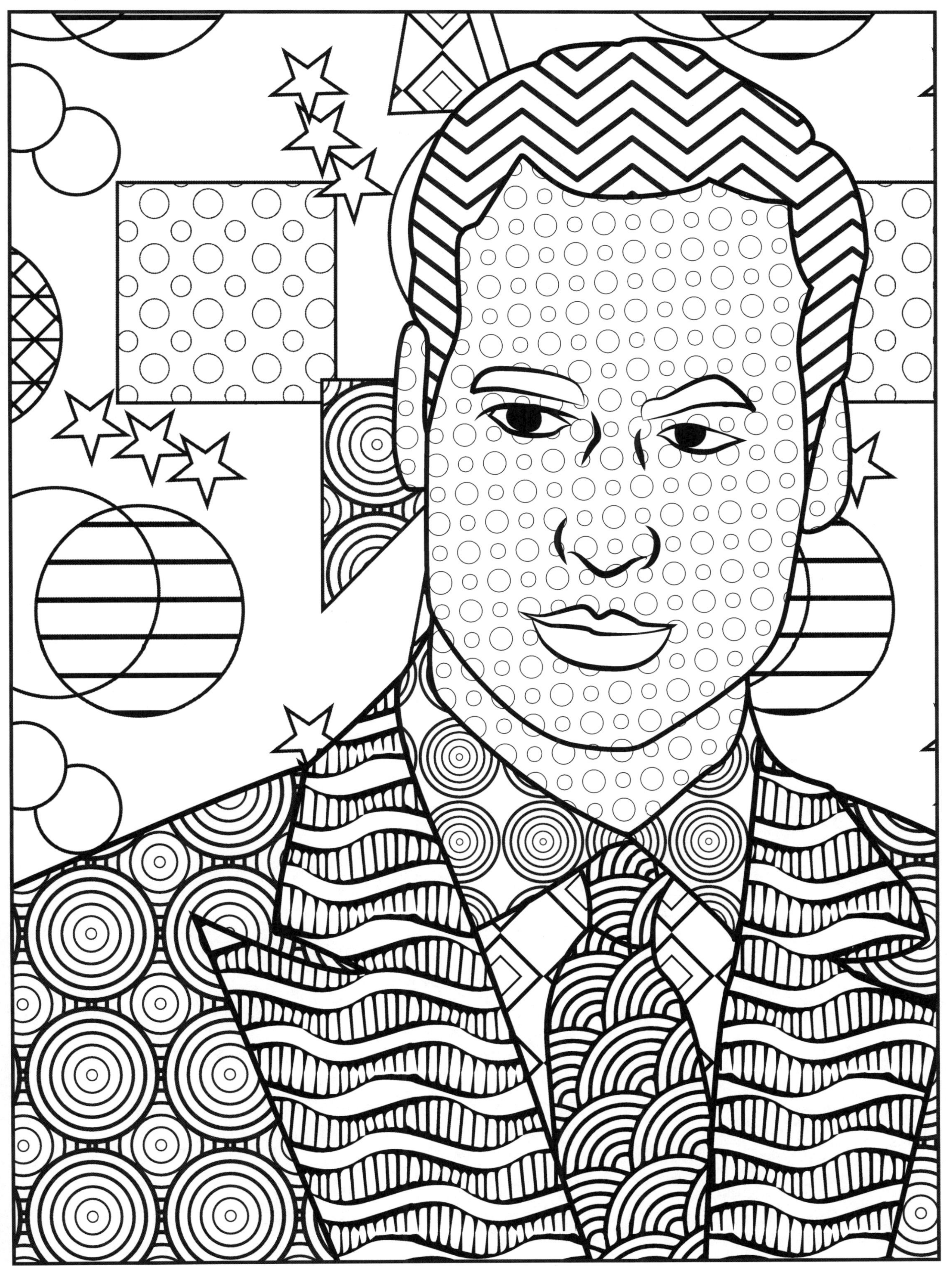

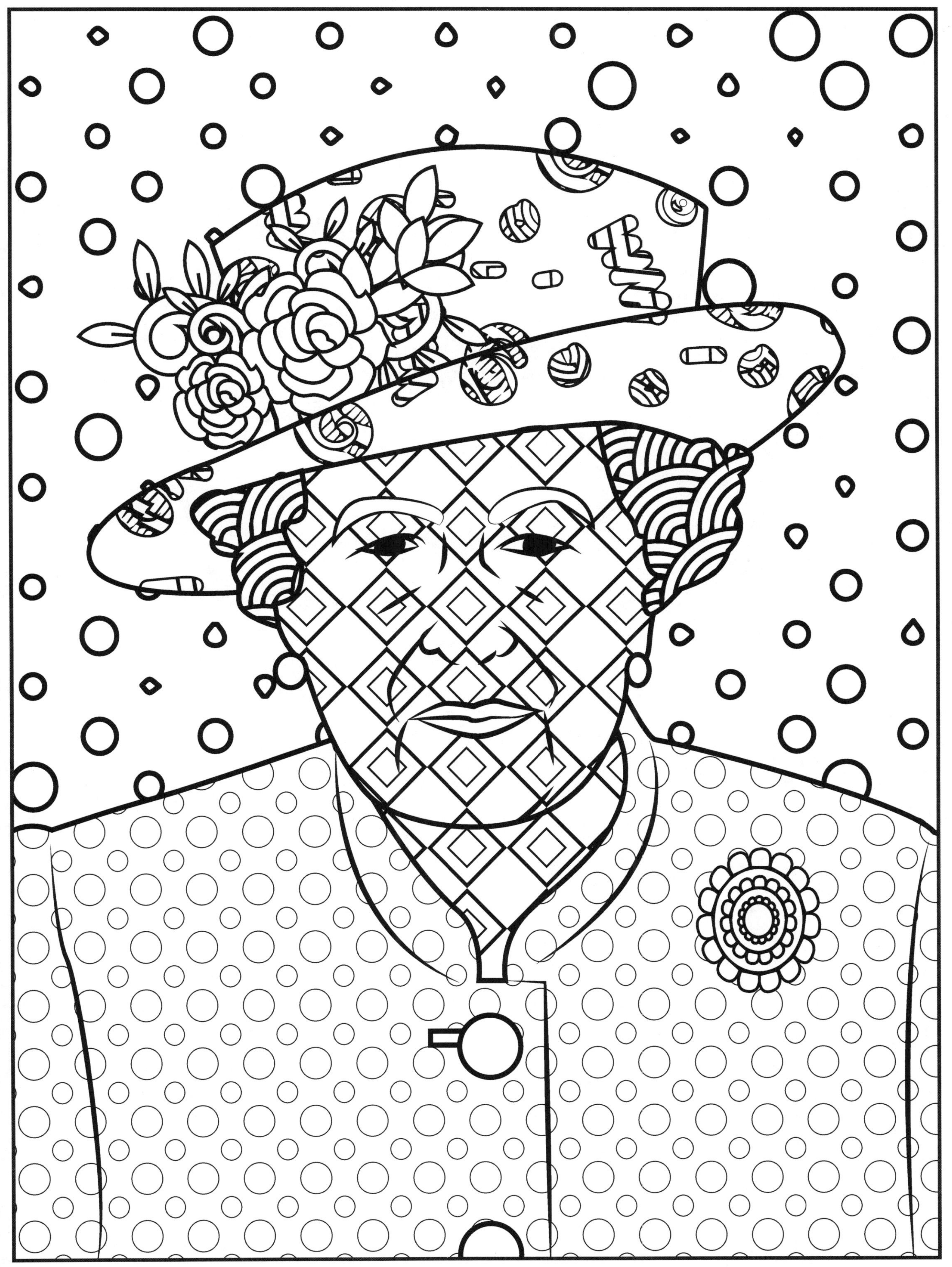

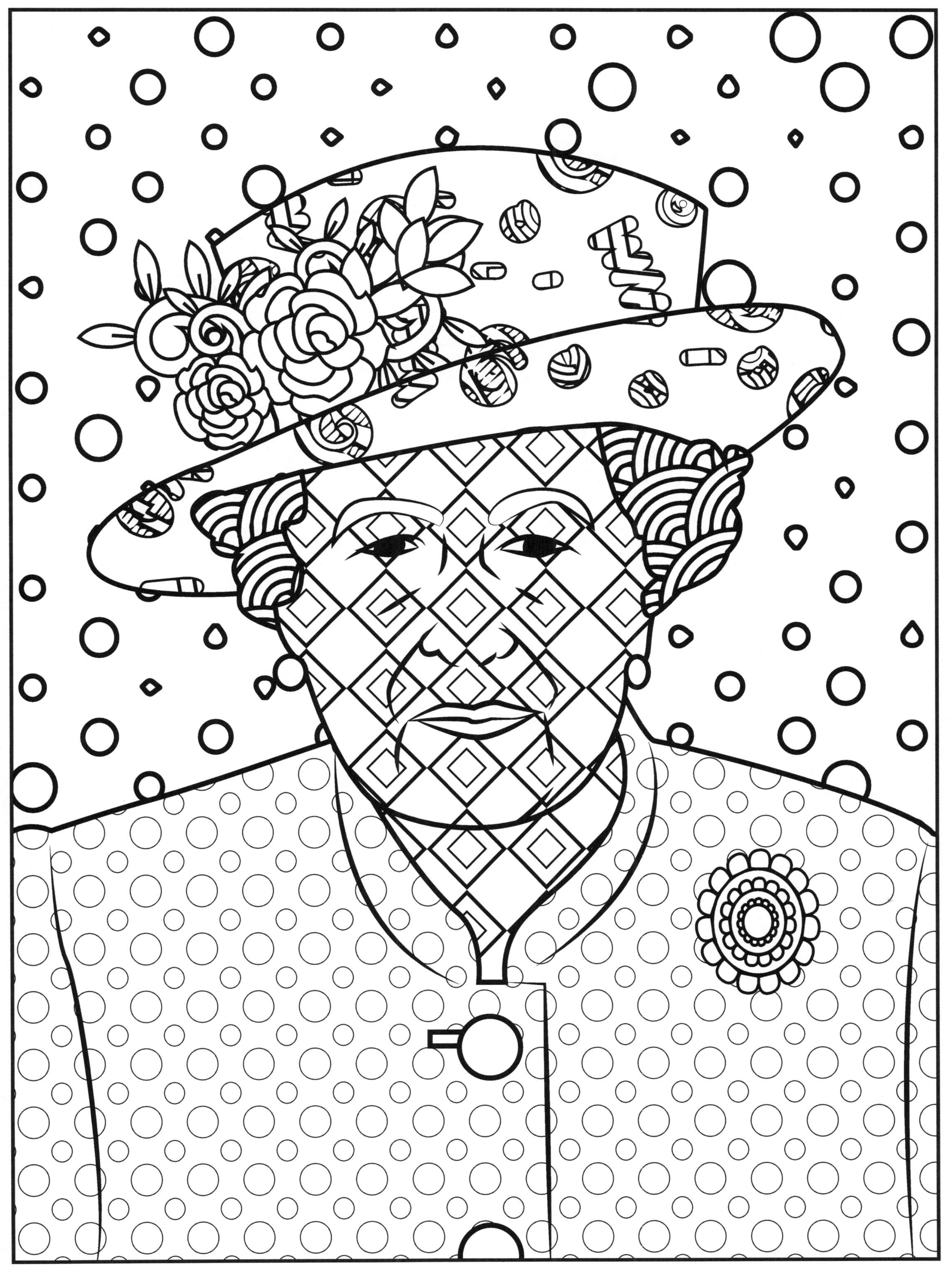

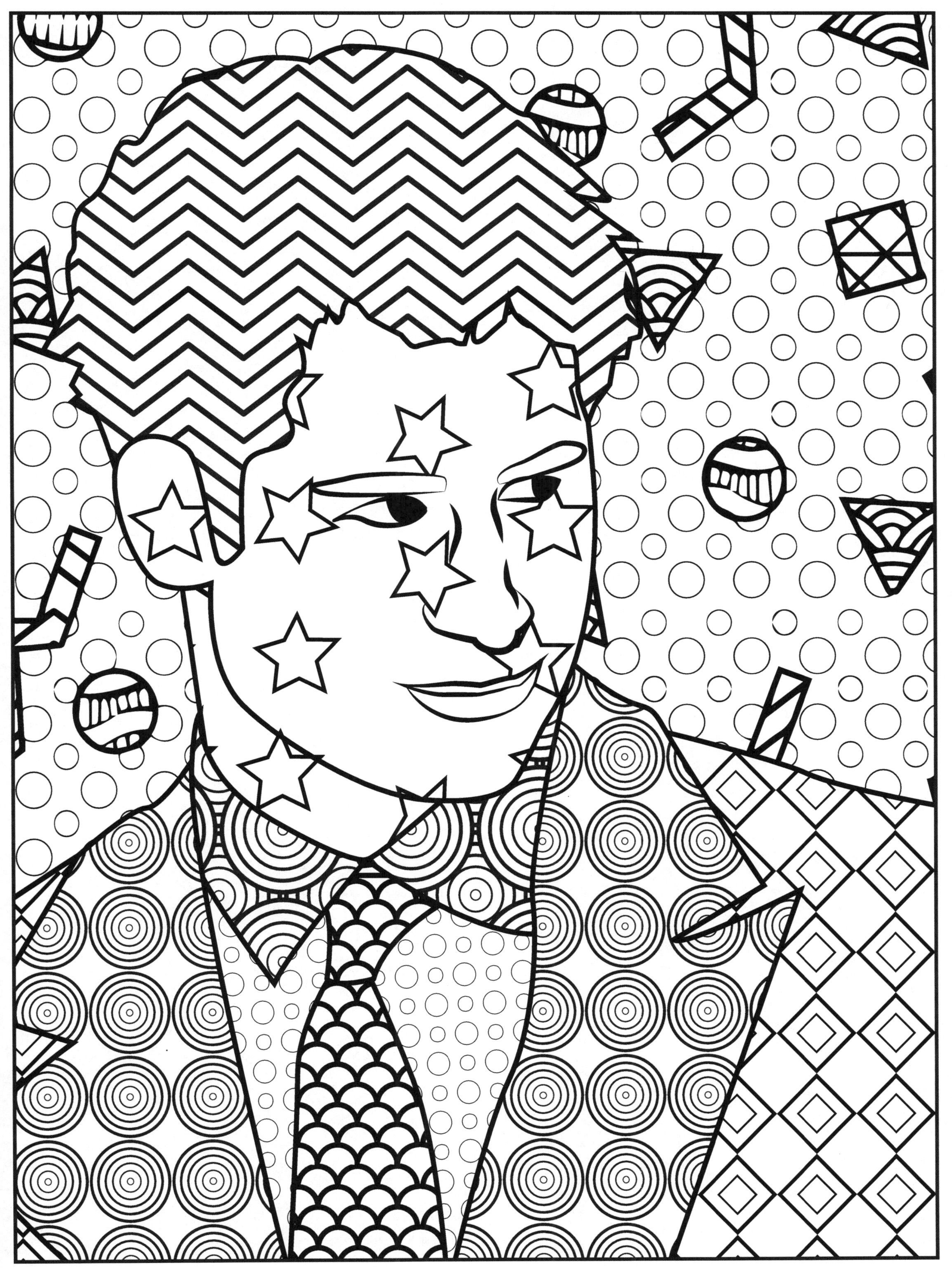

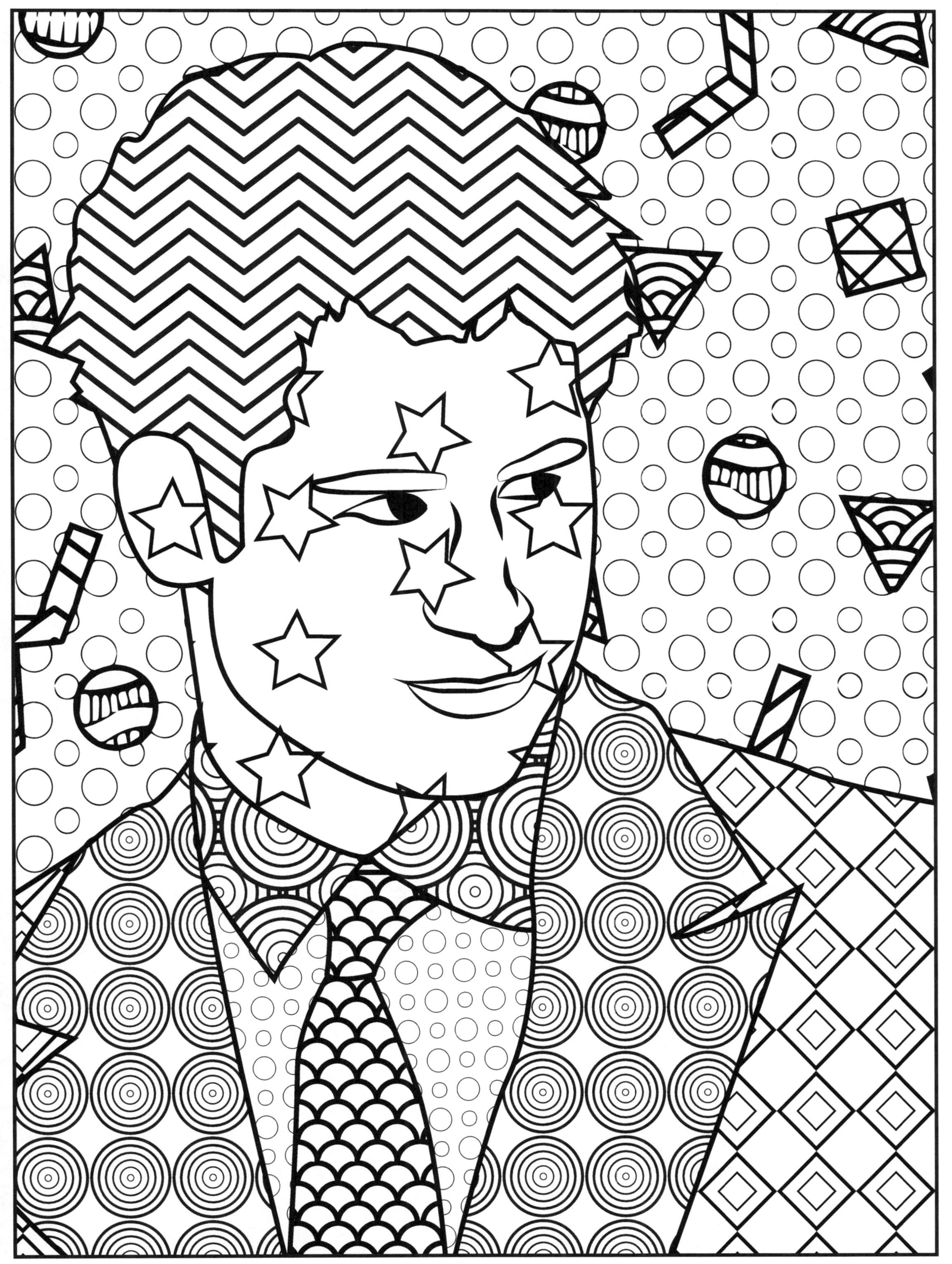

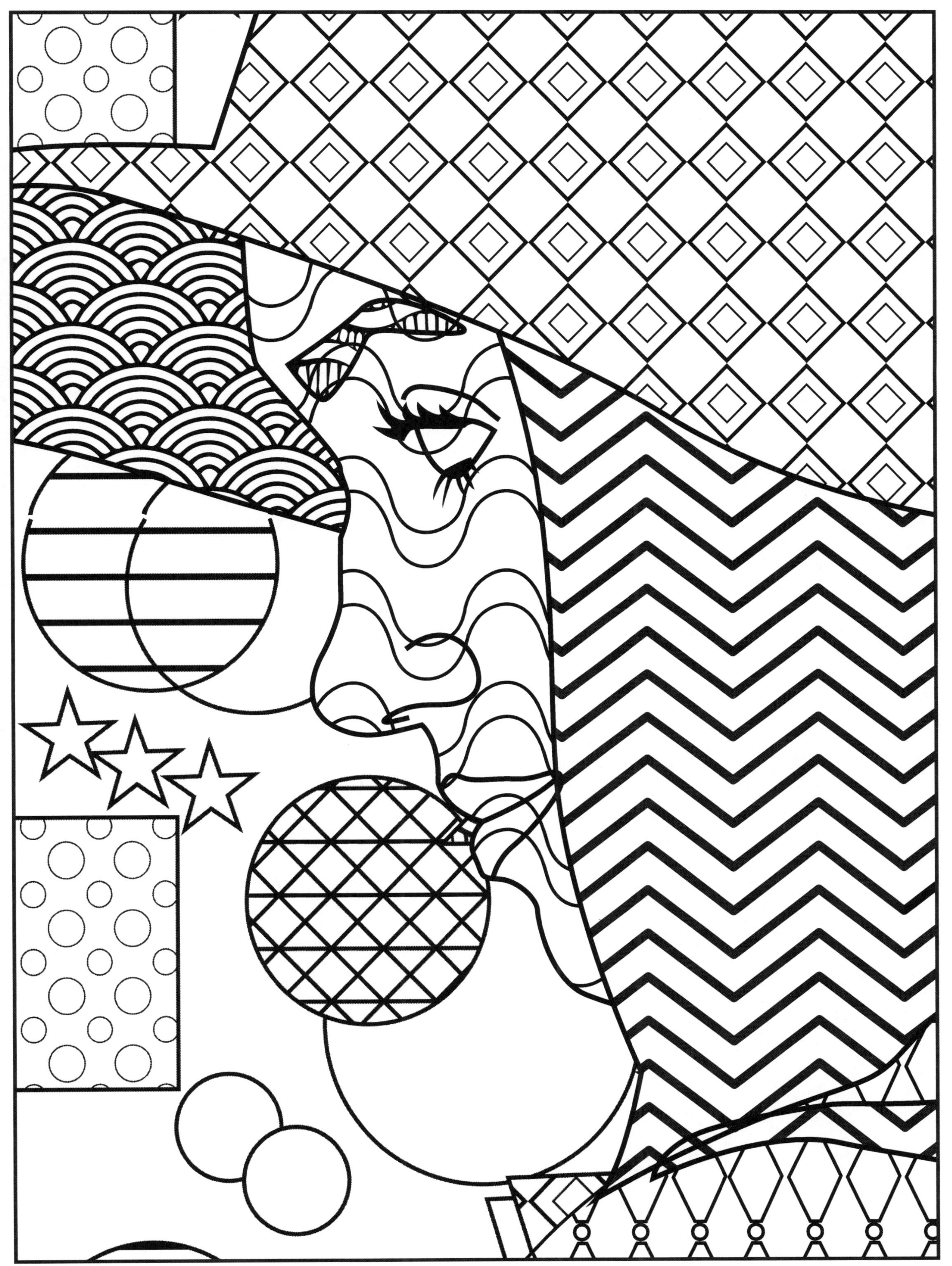

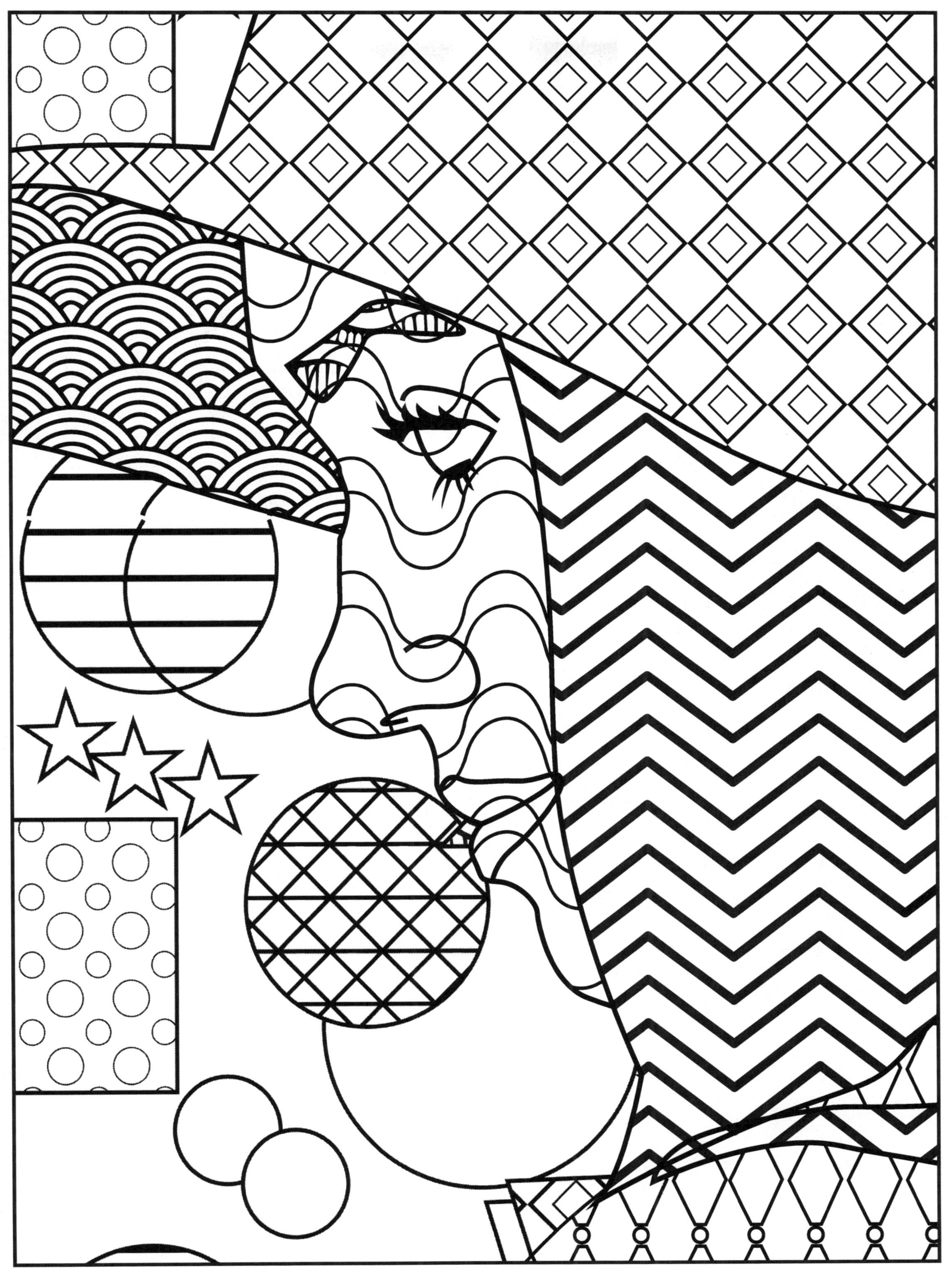

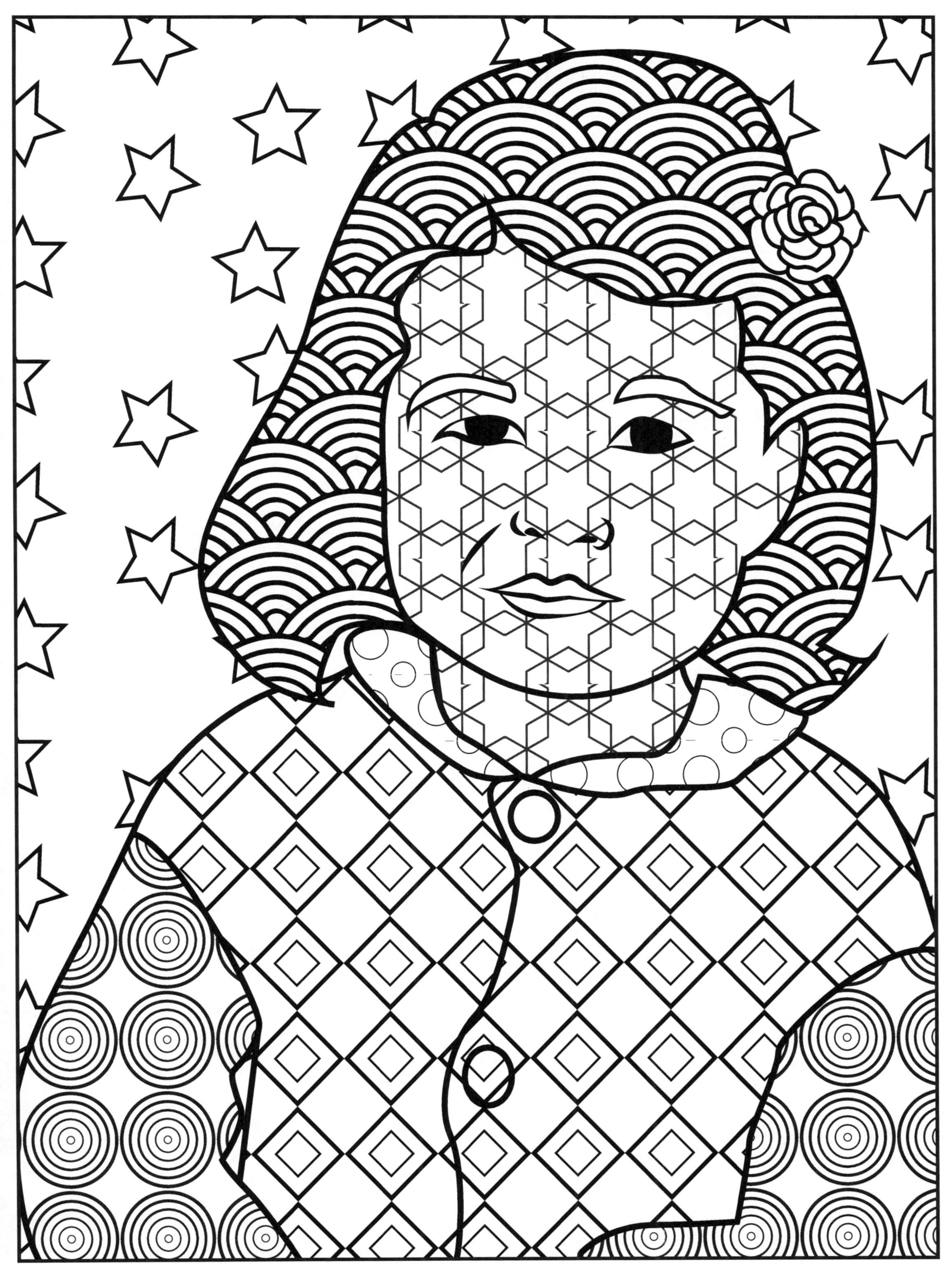

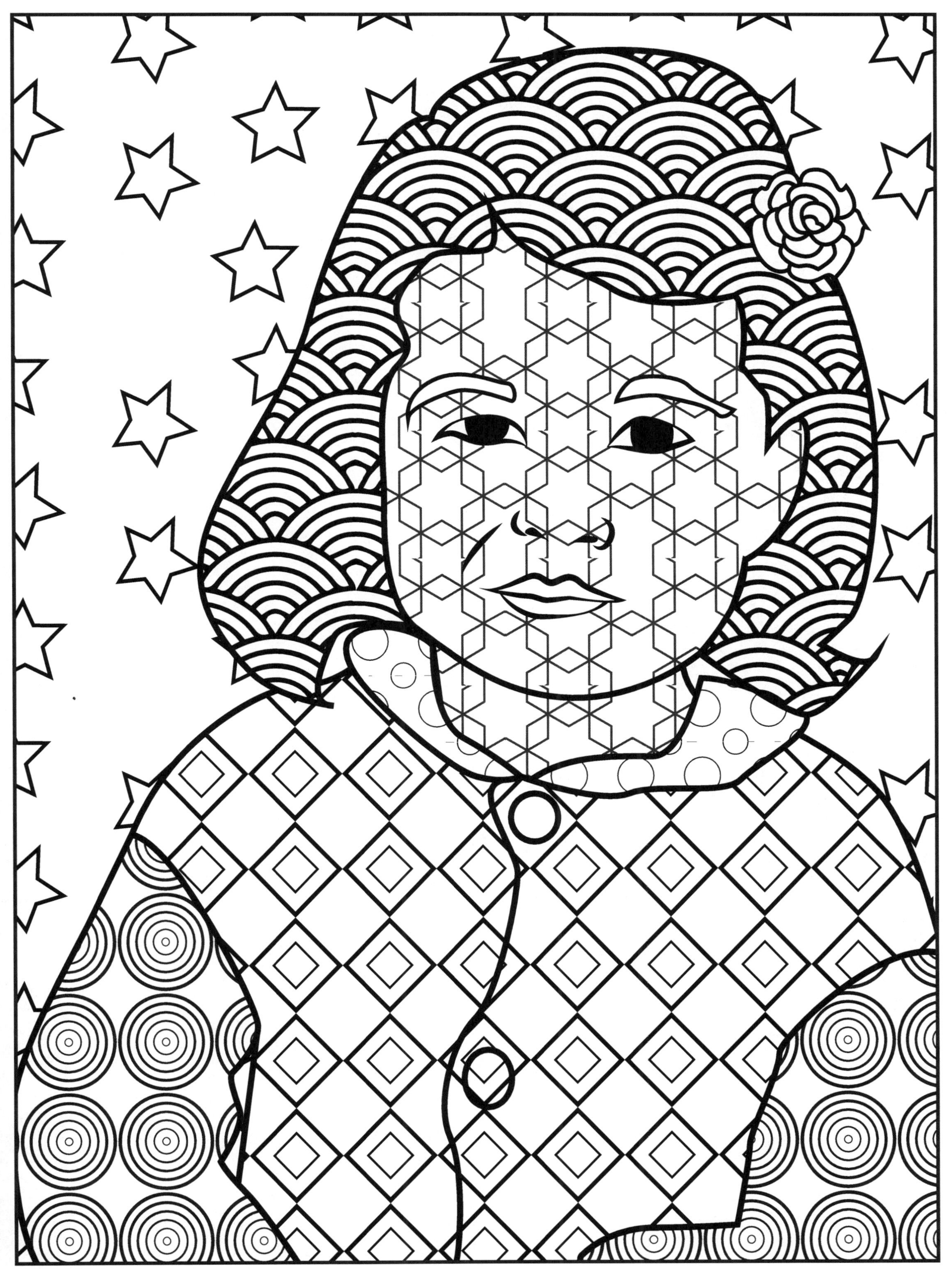

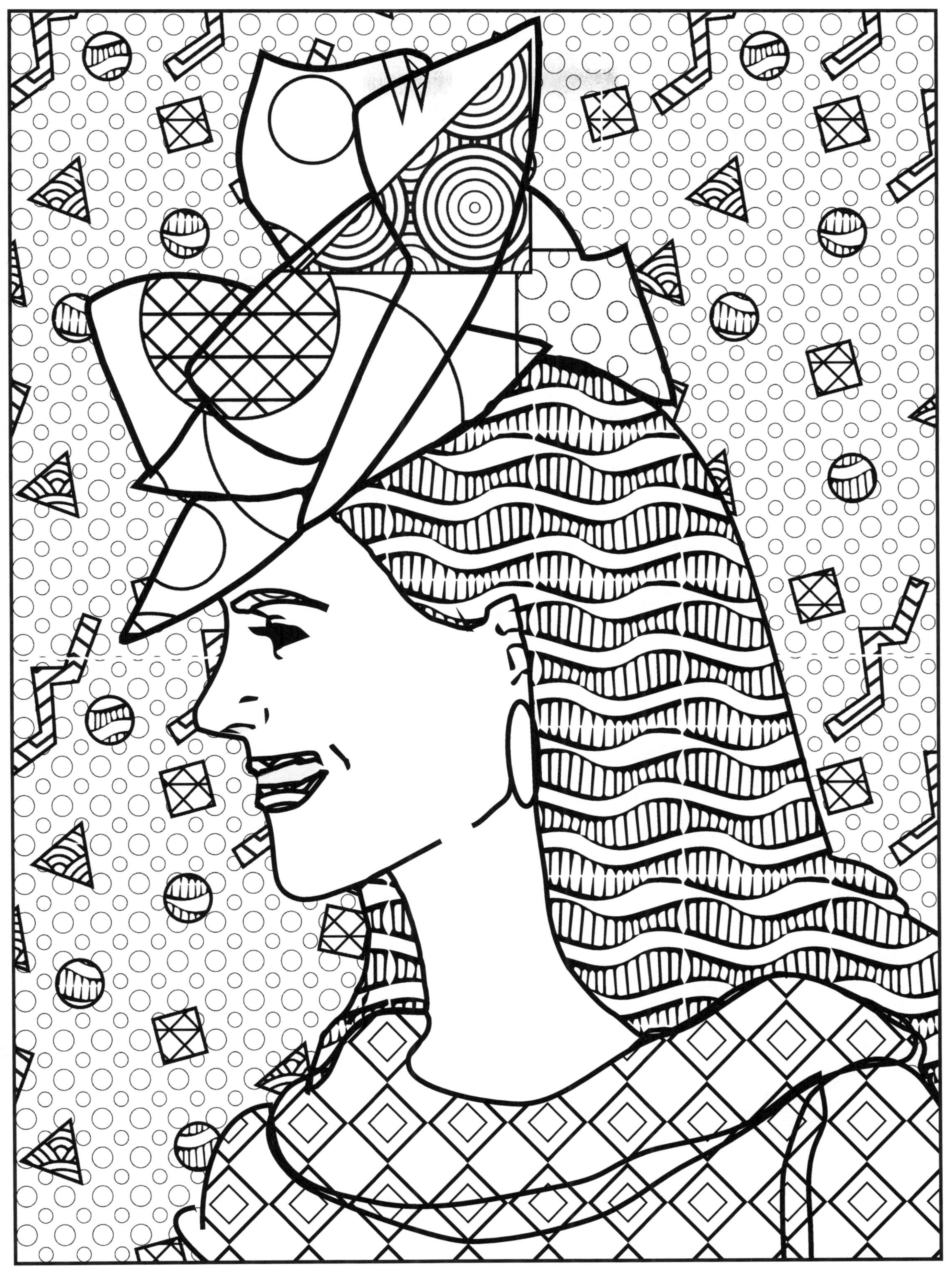

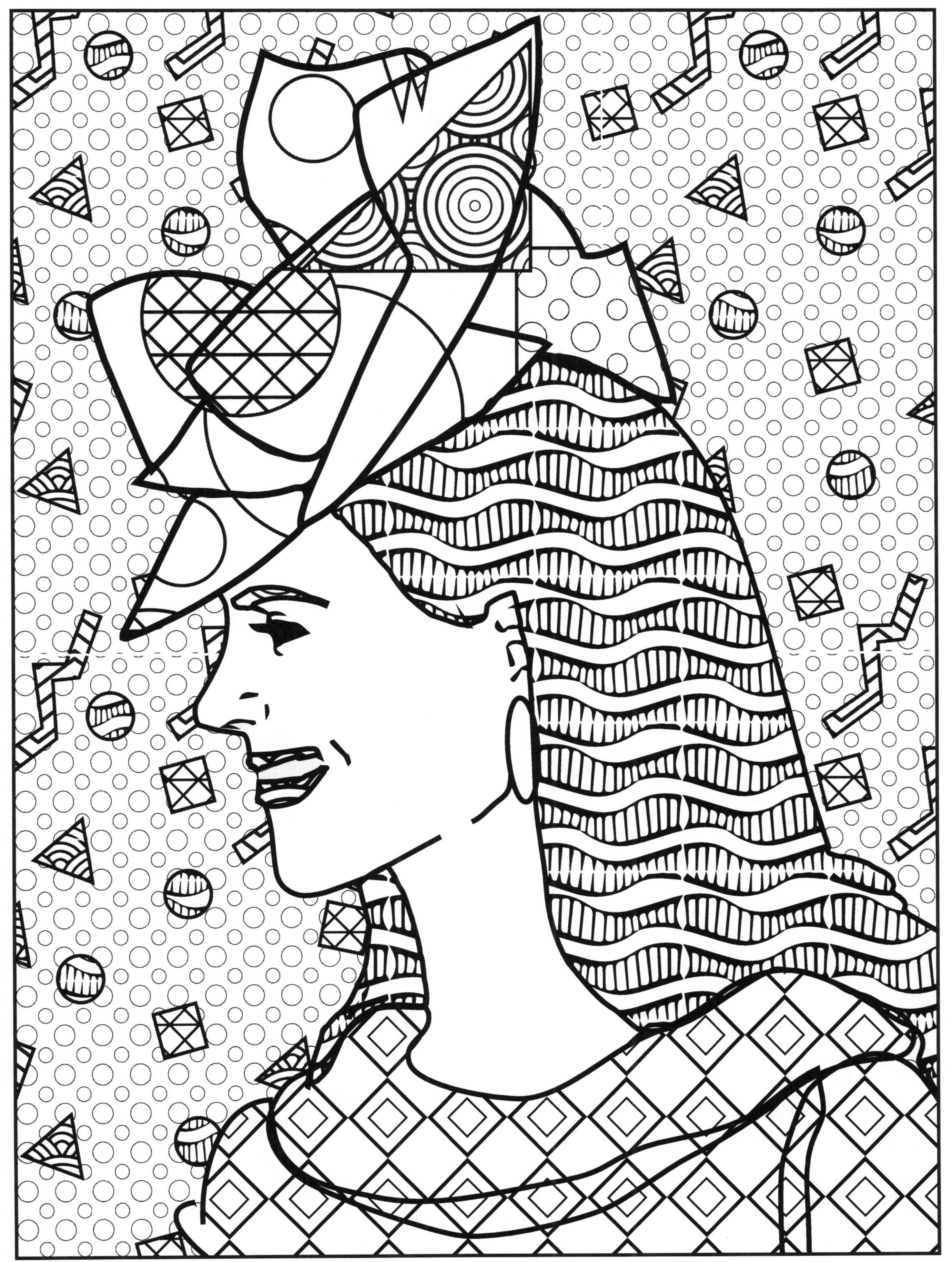

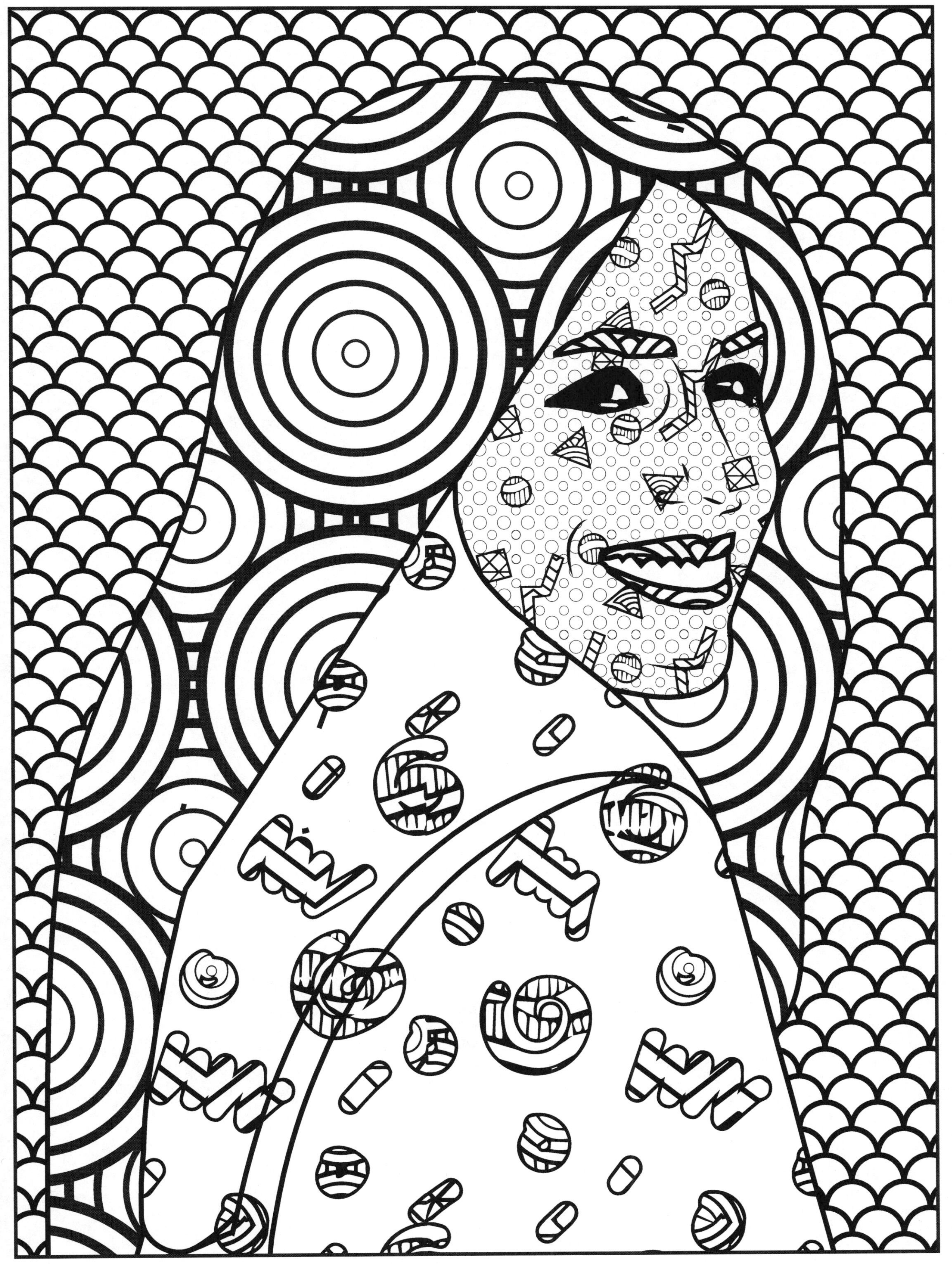

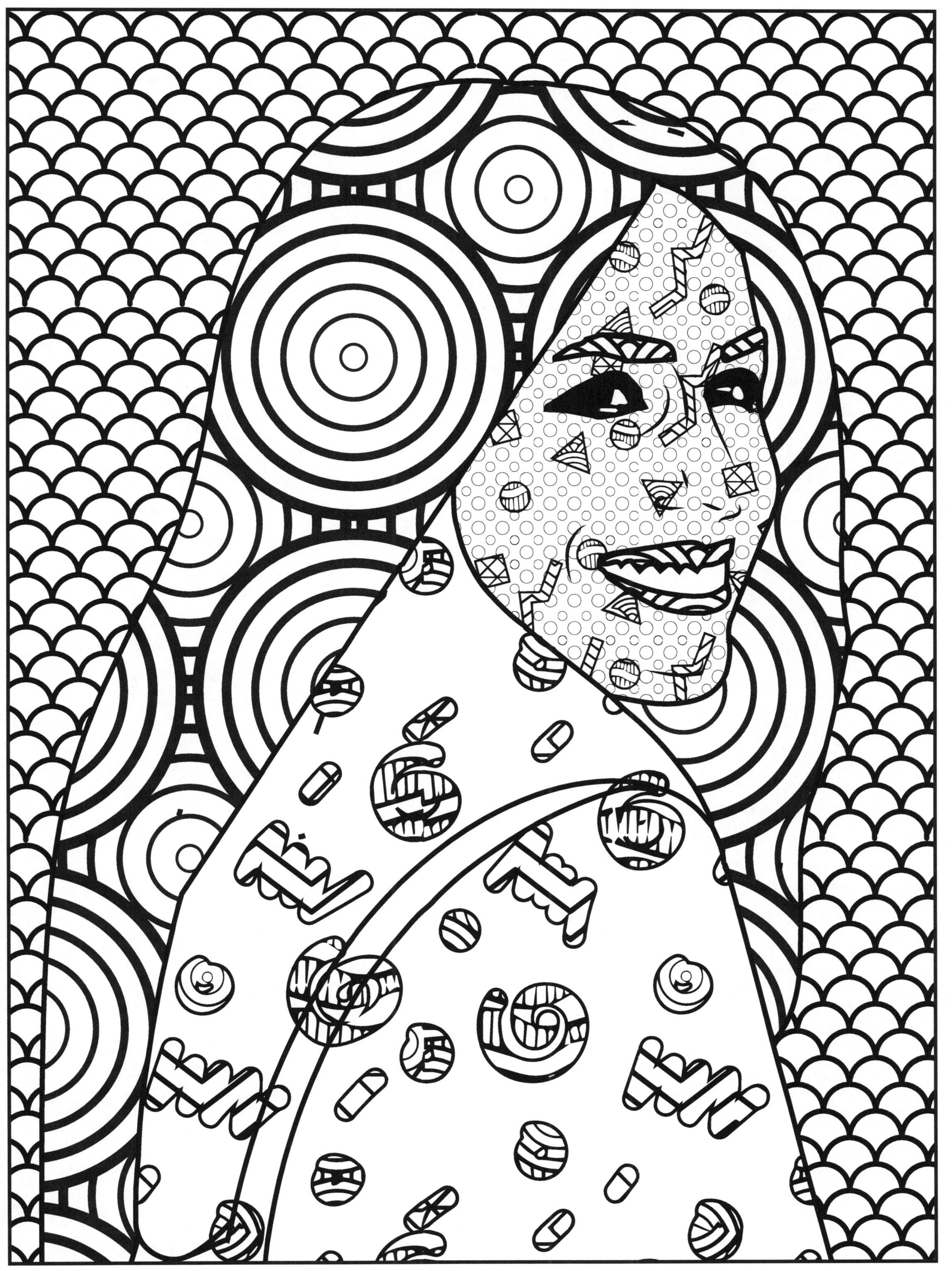

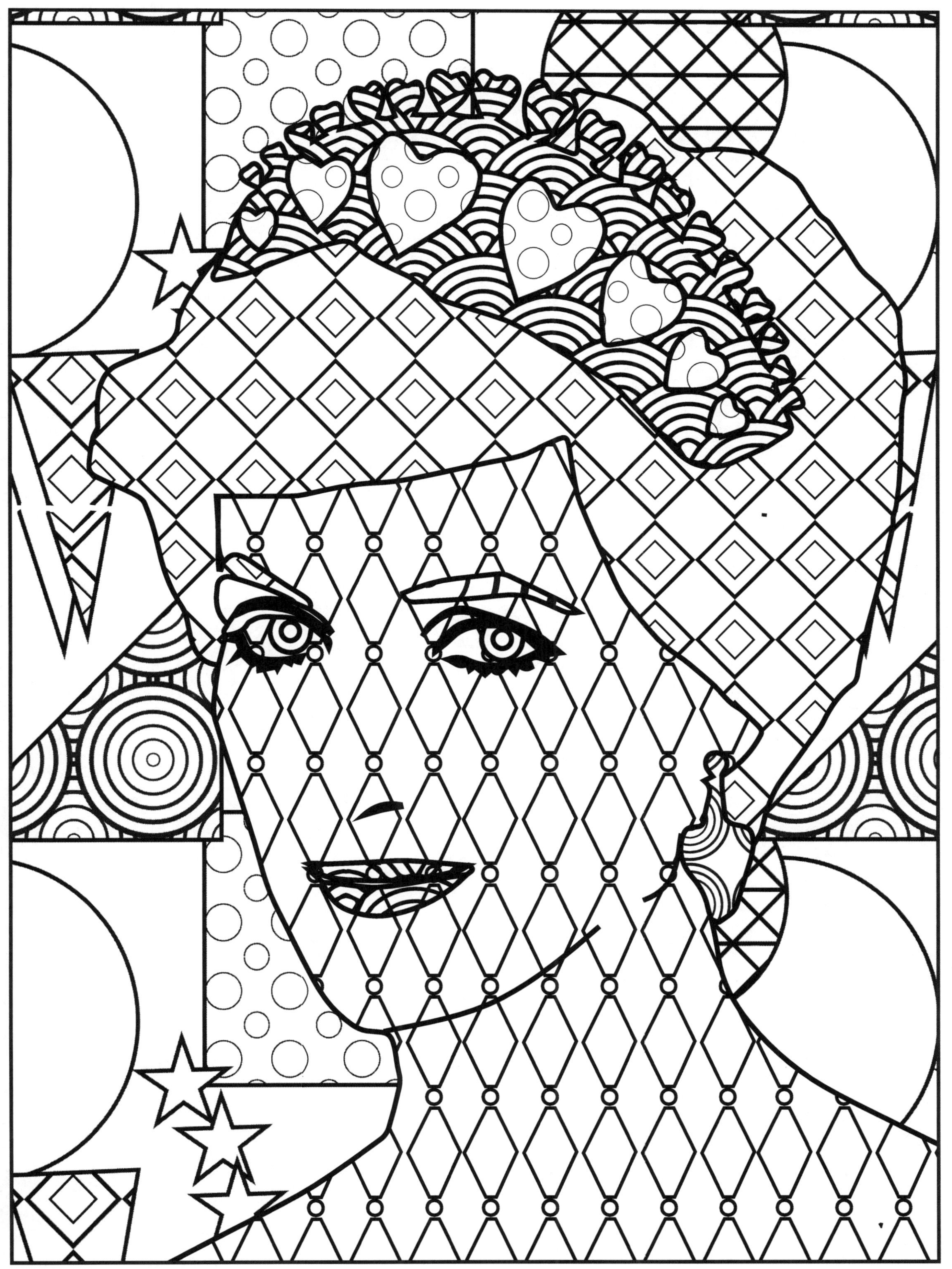

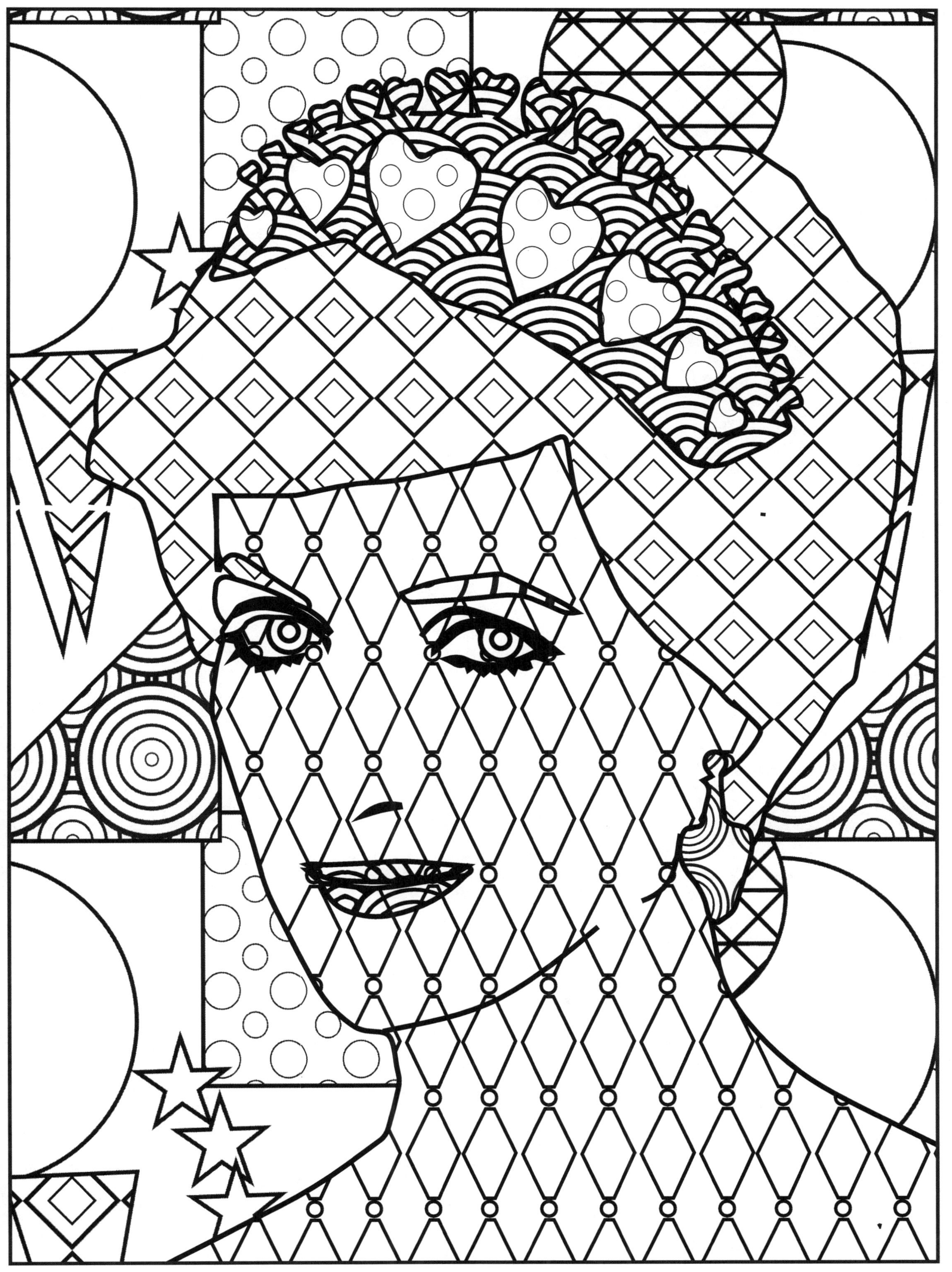

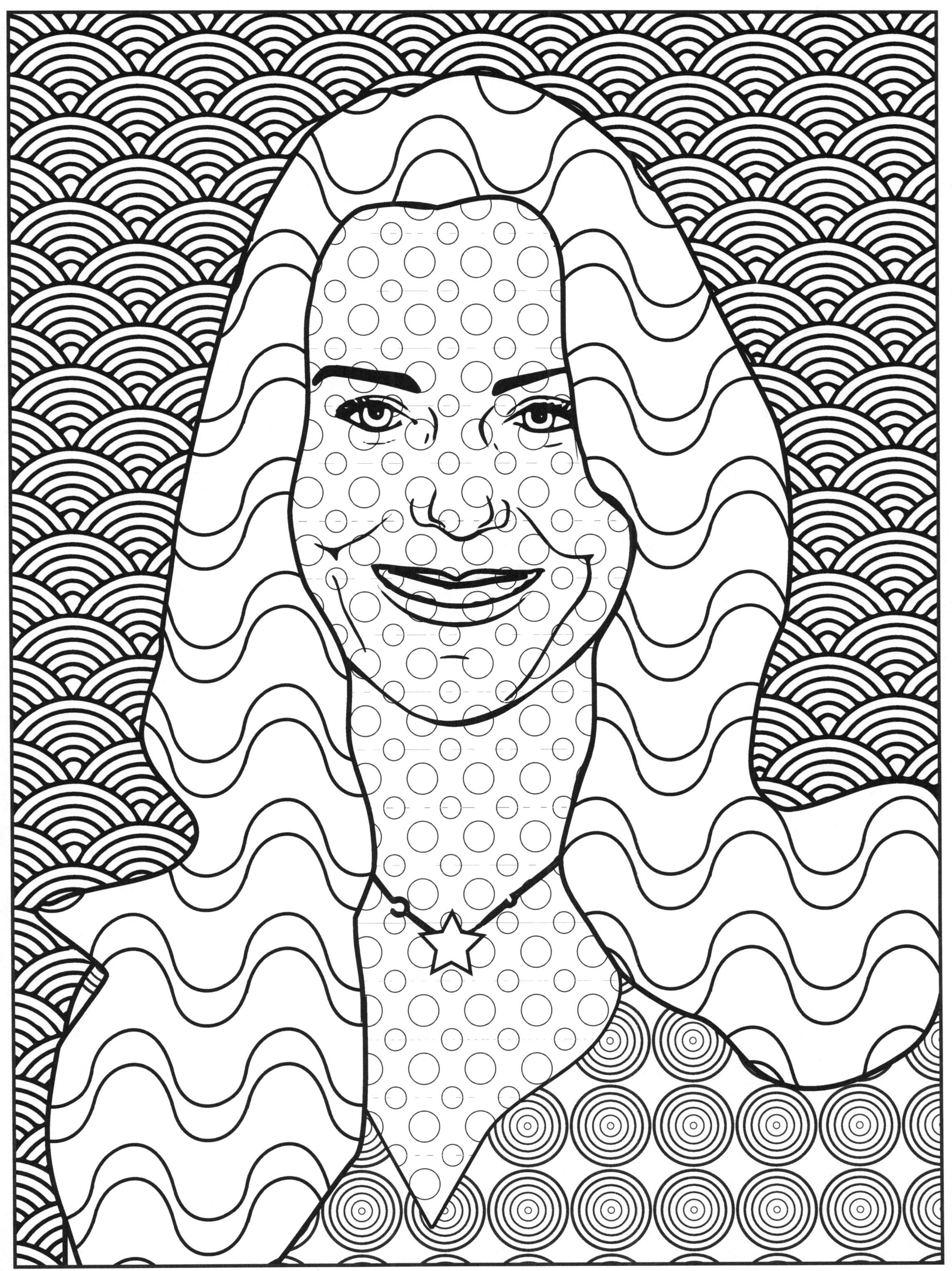

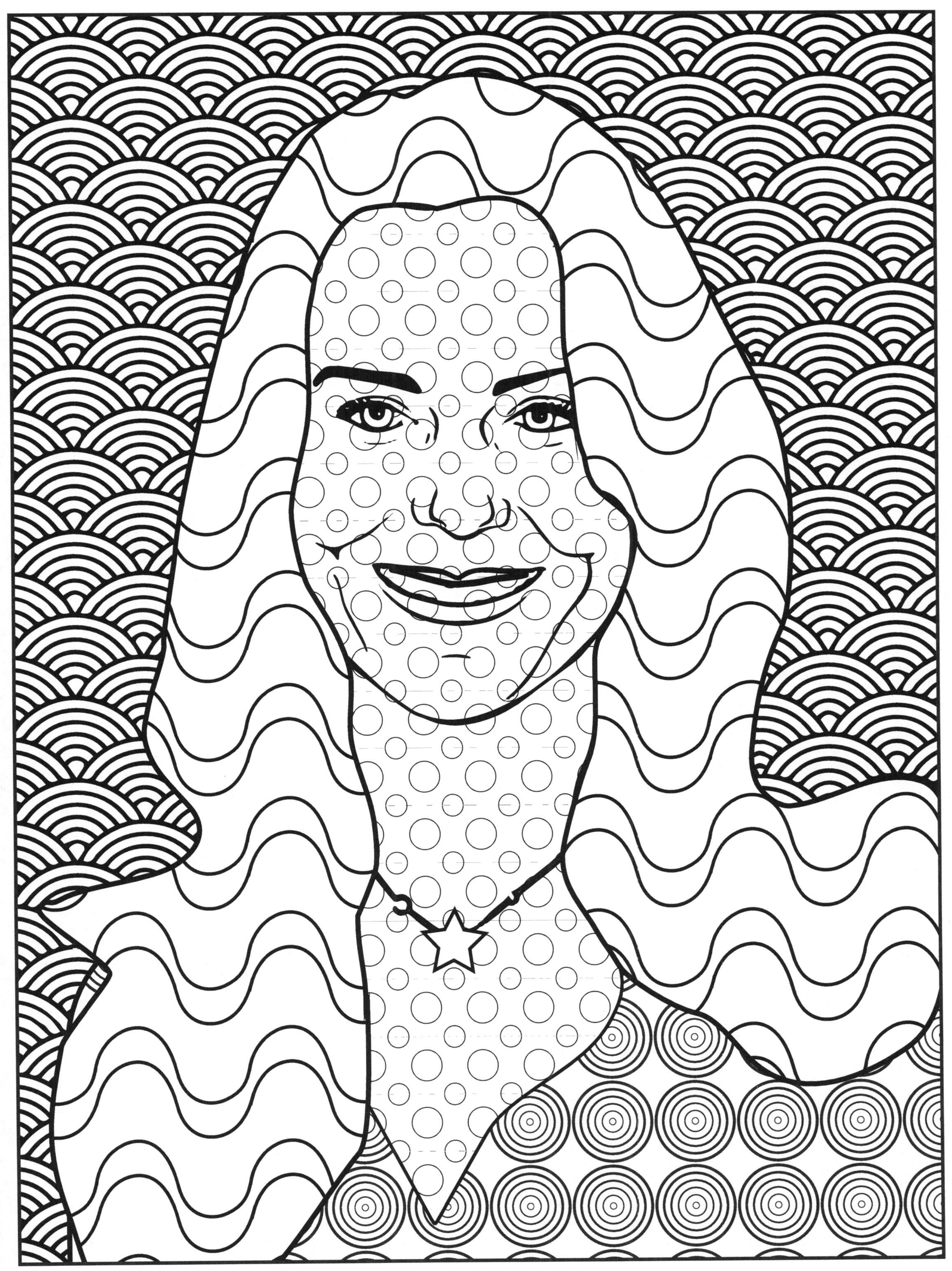

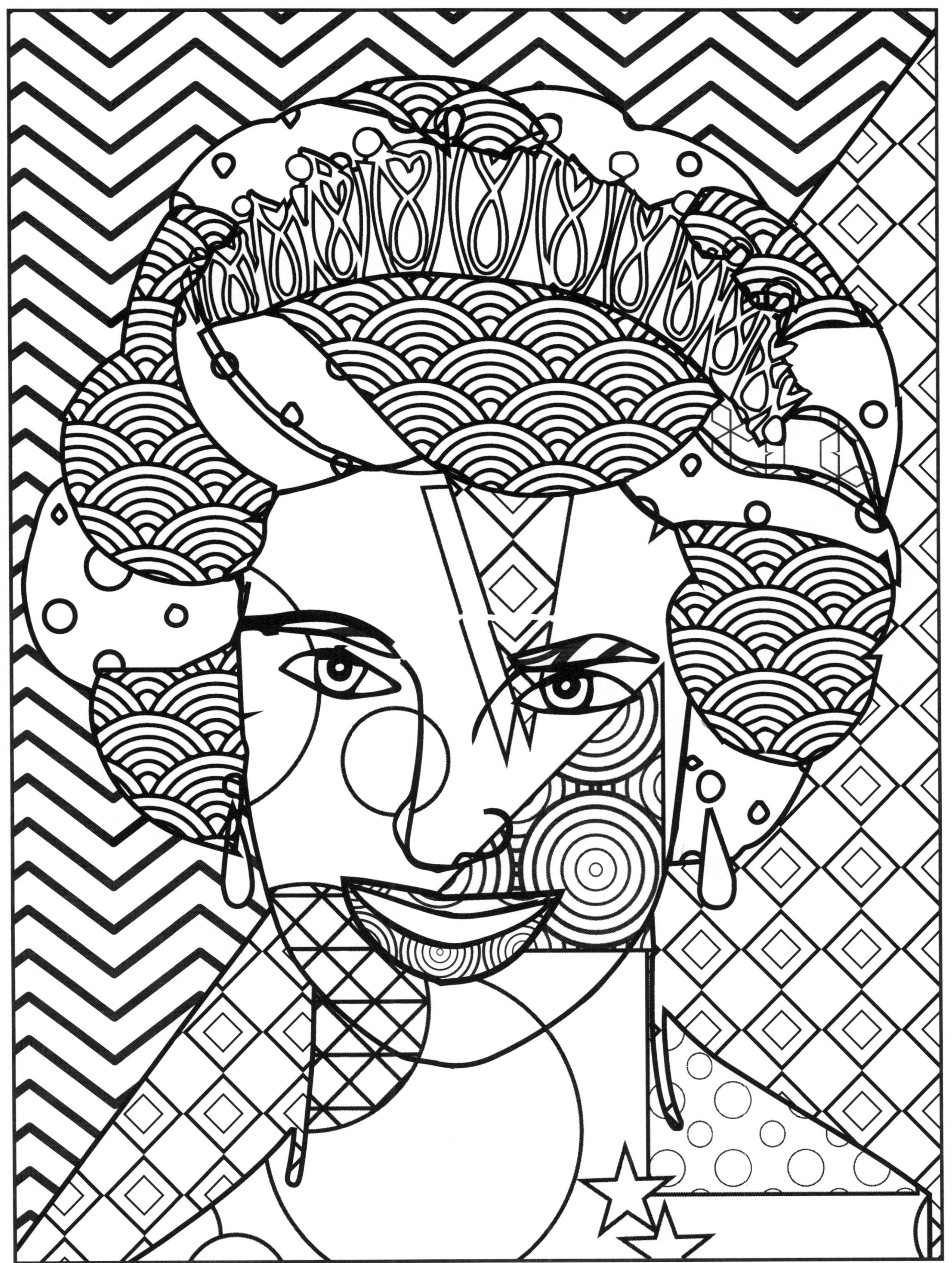

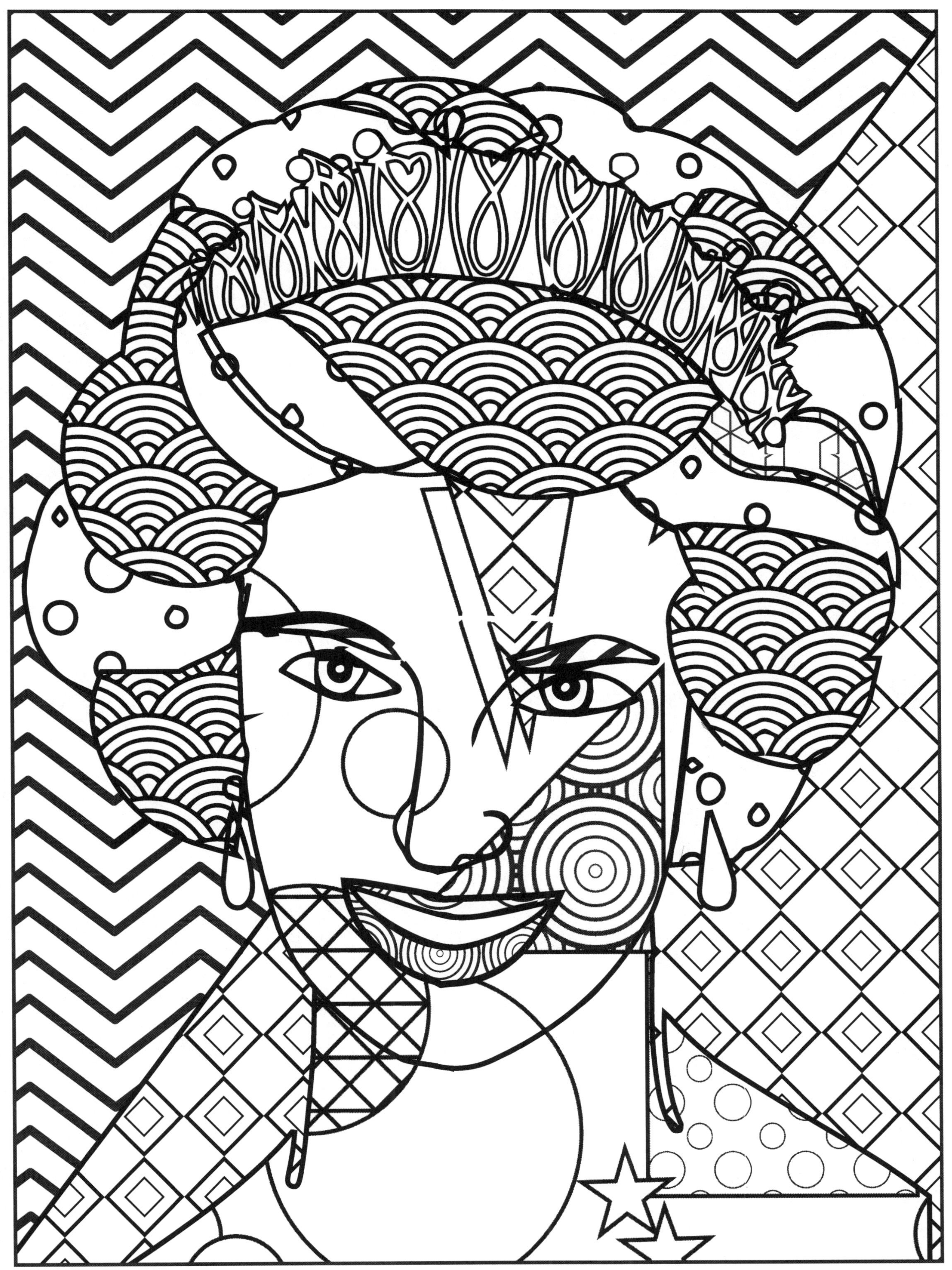

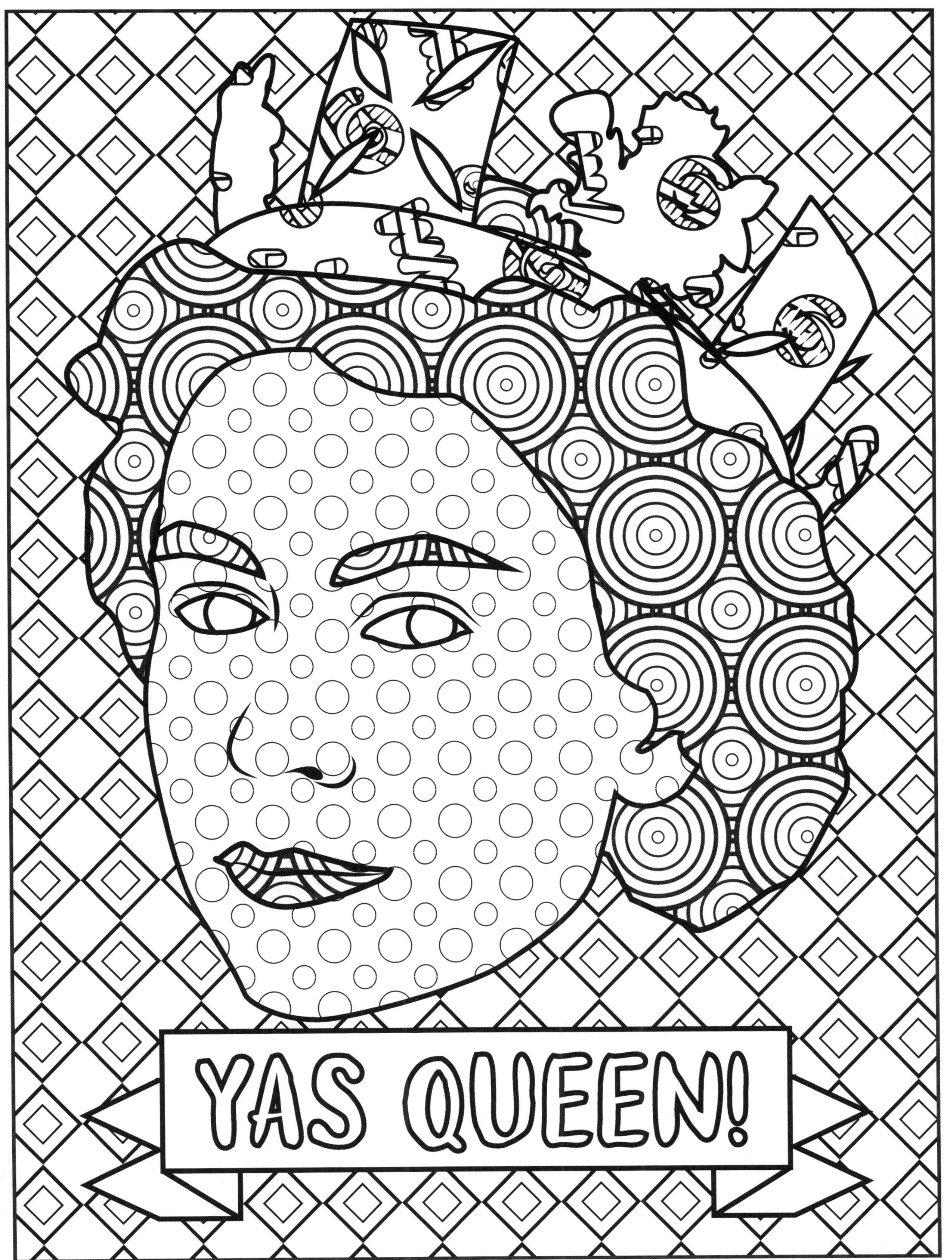
YAS QUEEN!

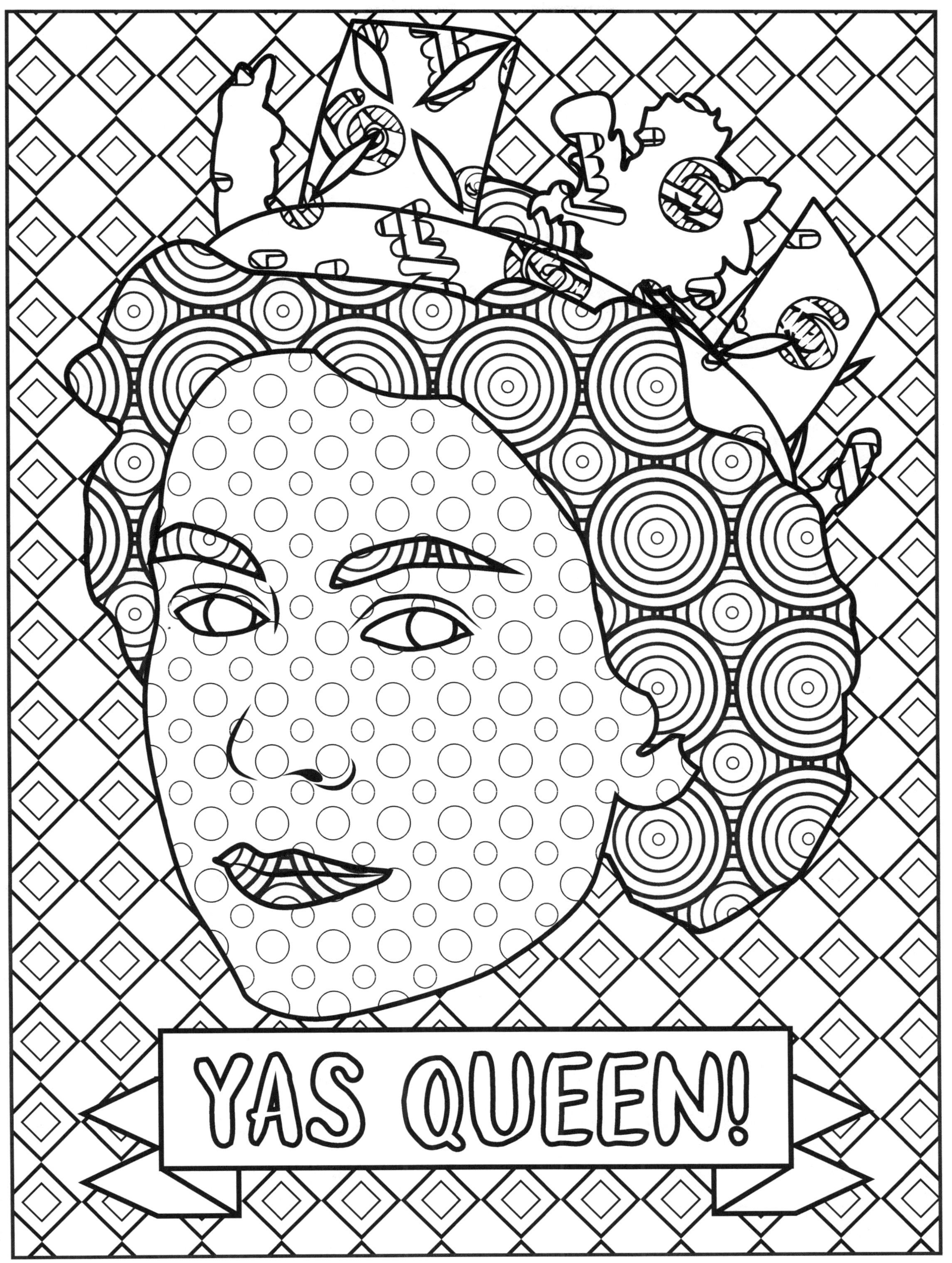
YAS QUEEN!

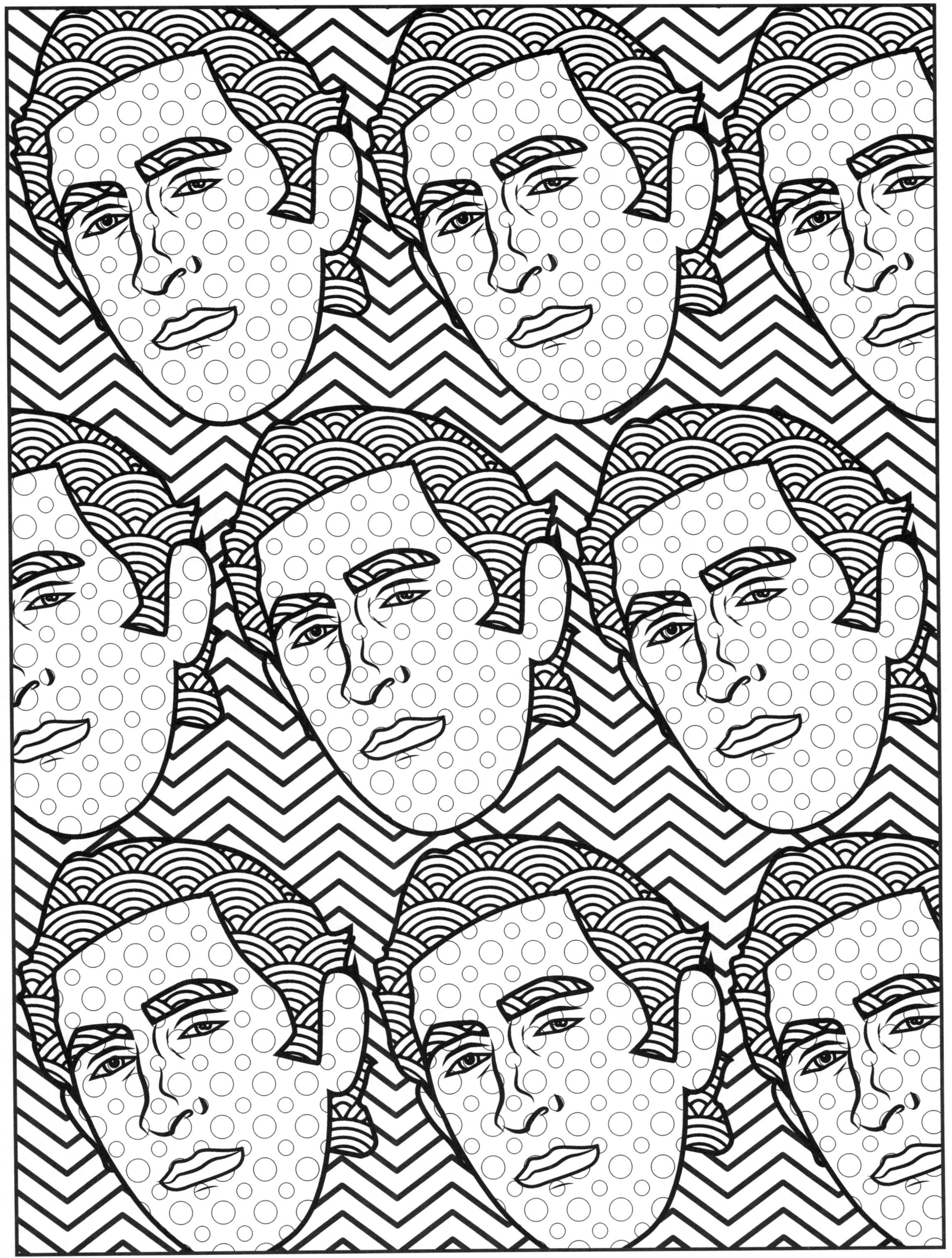

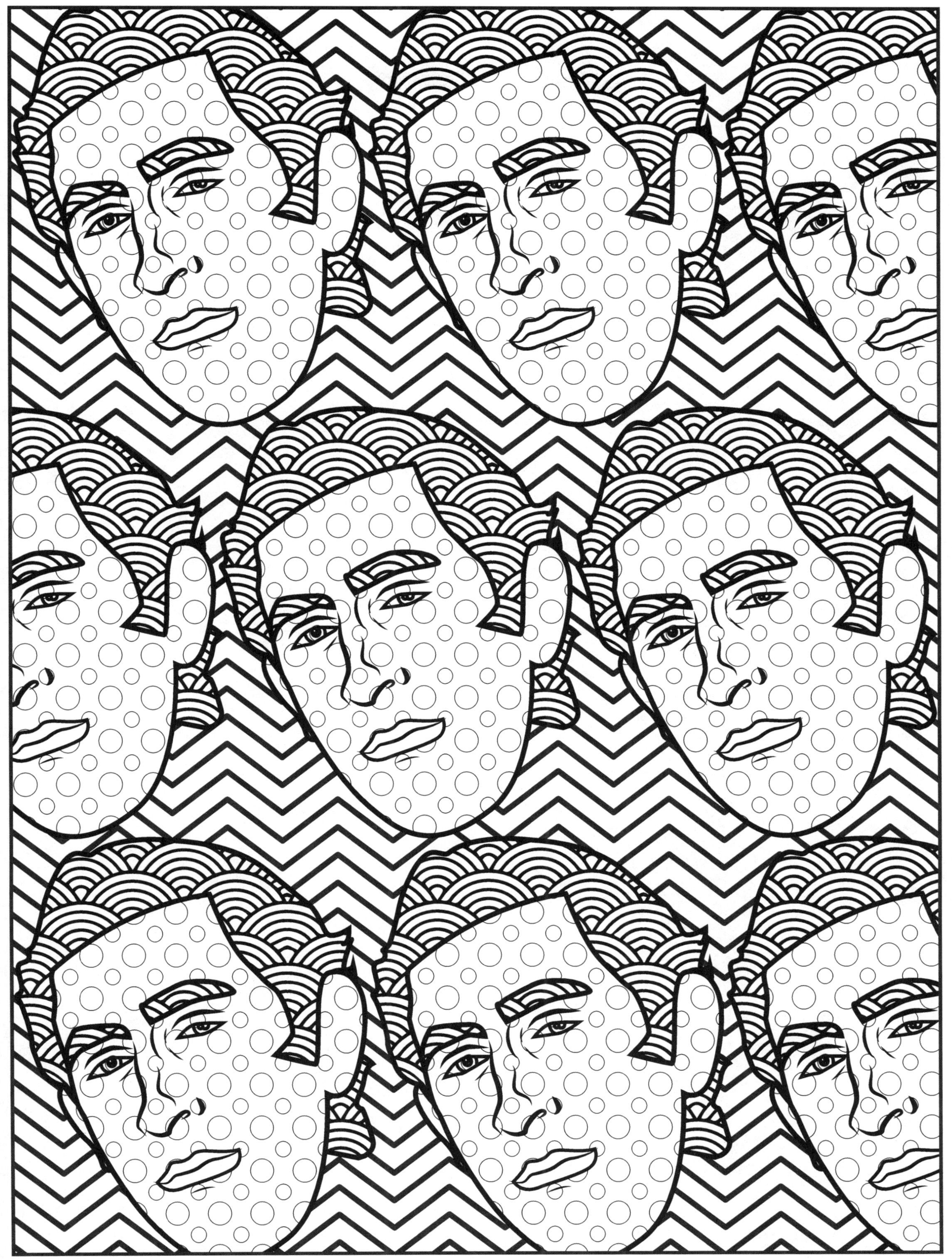

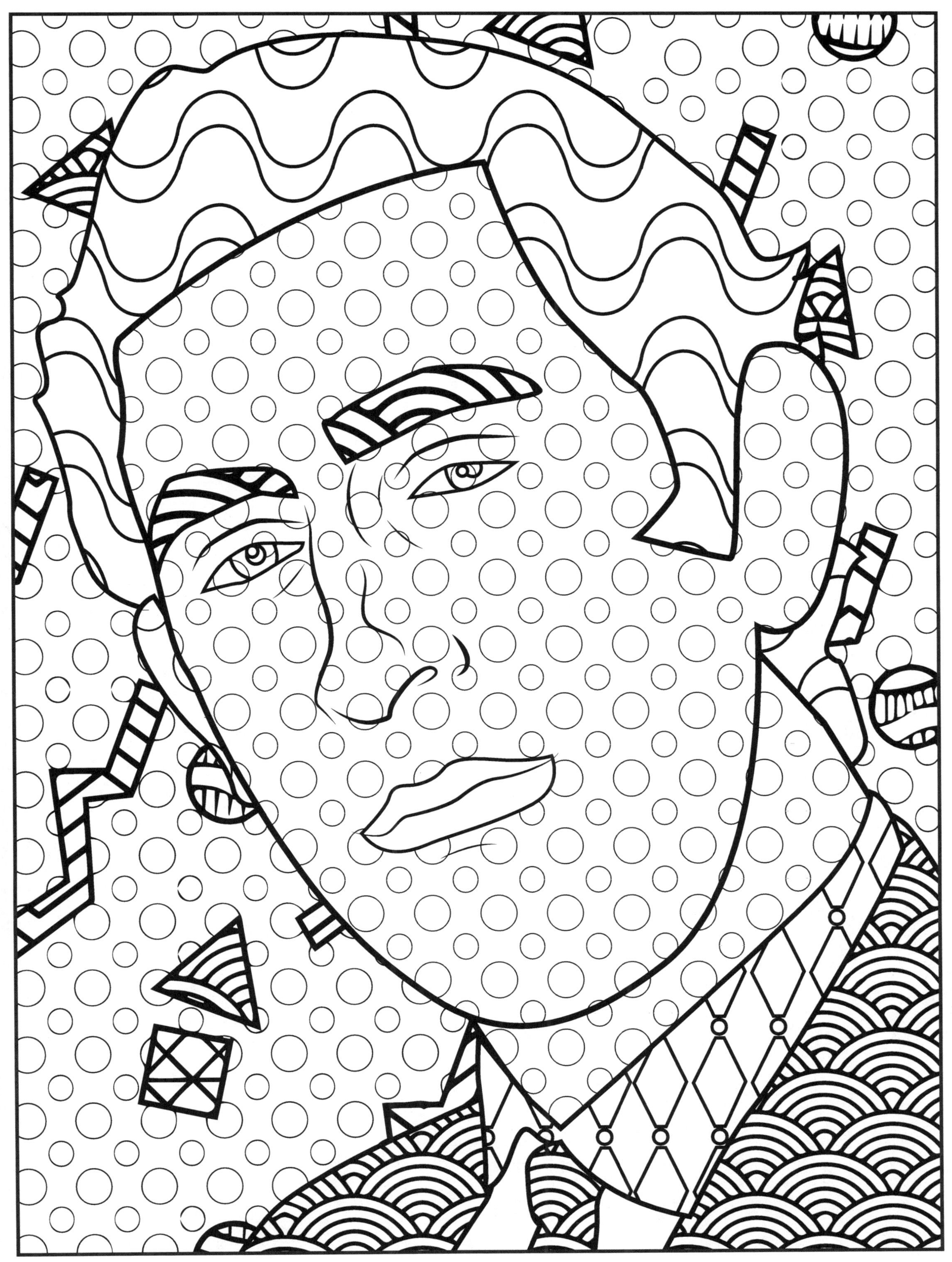

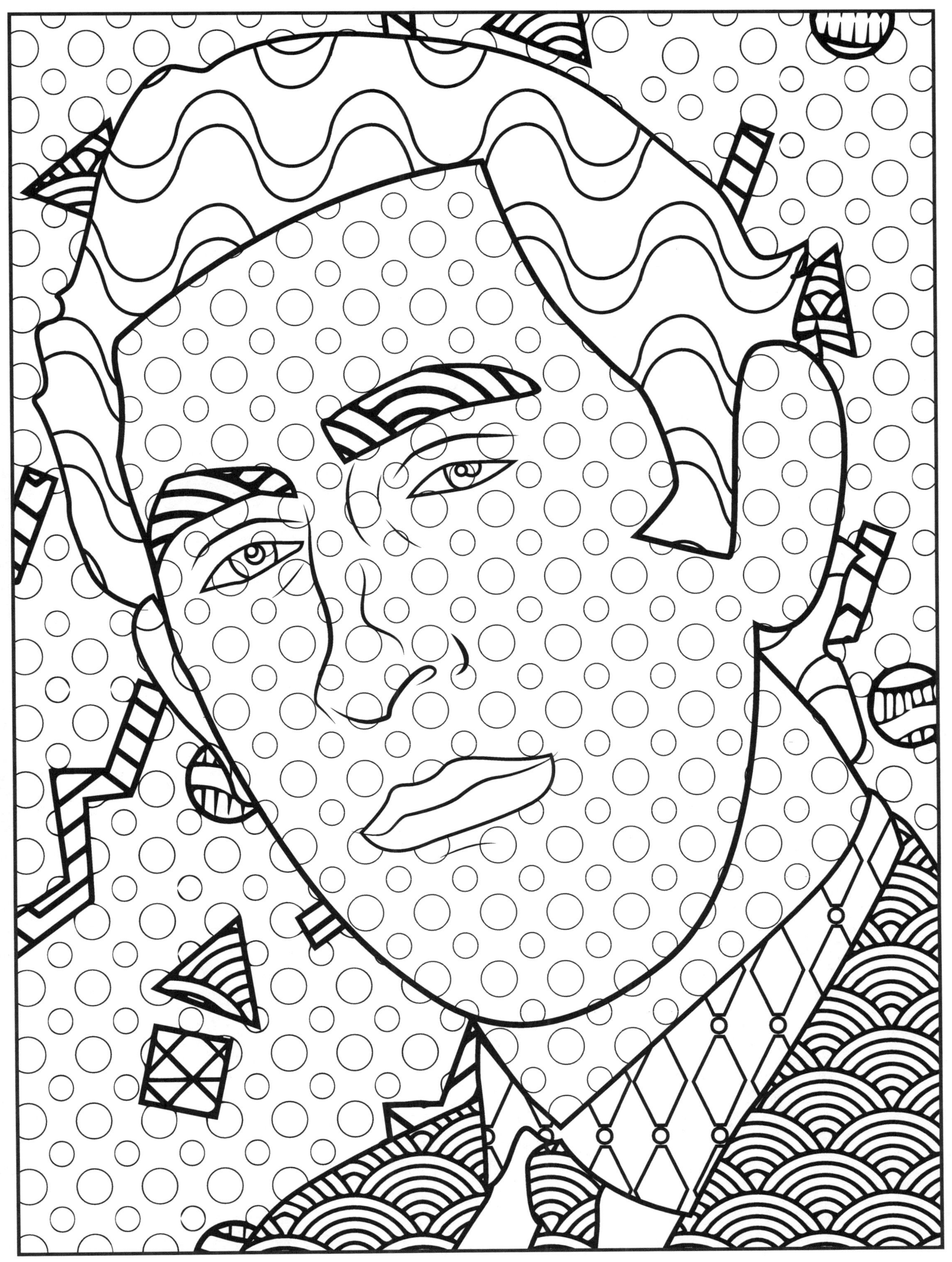

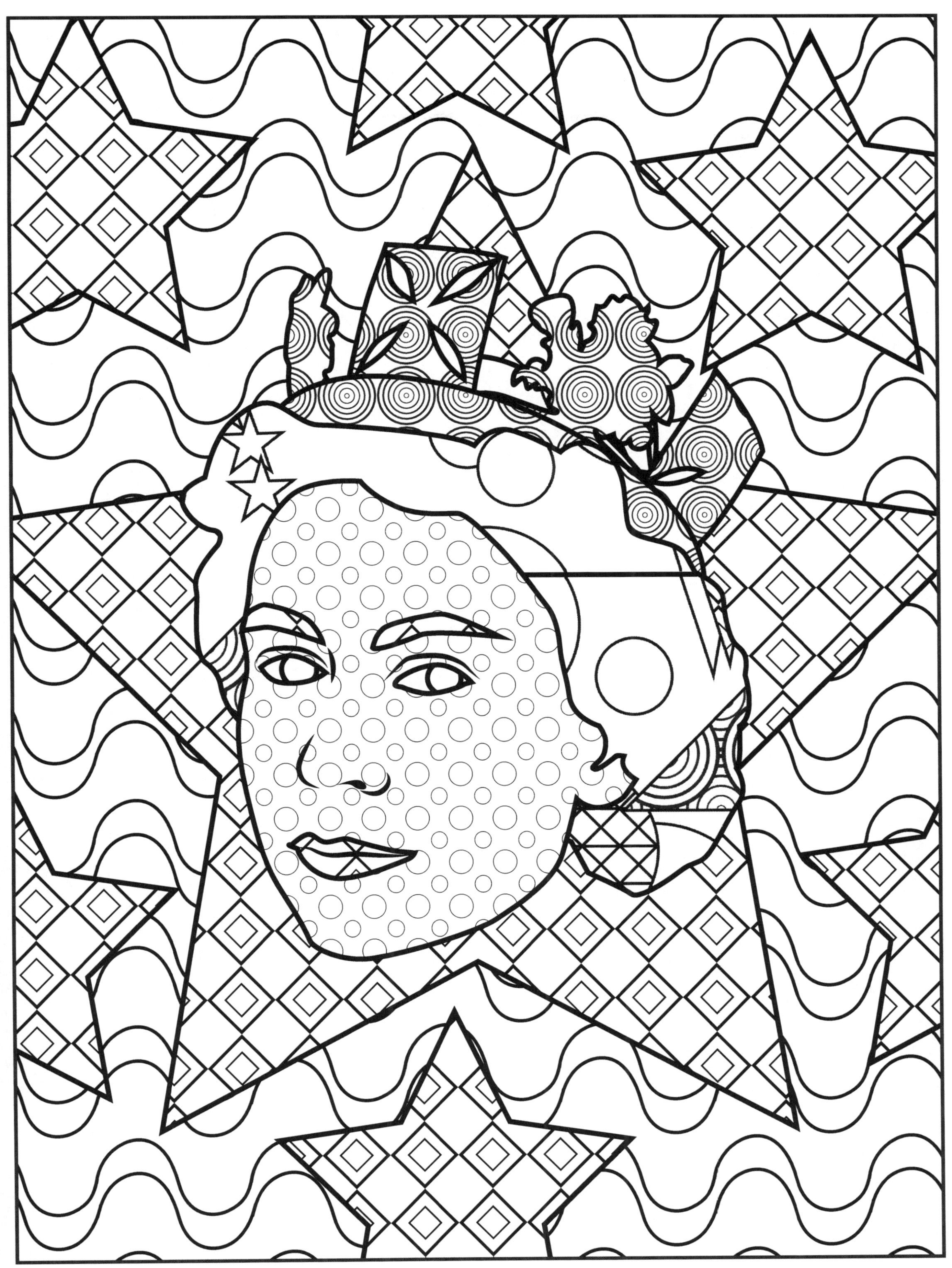

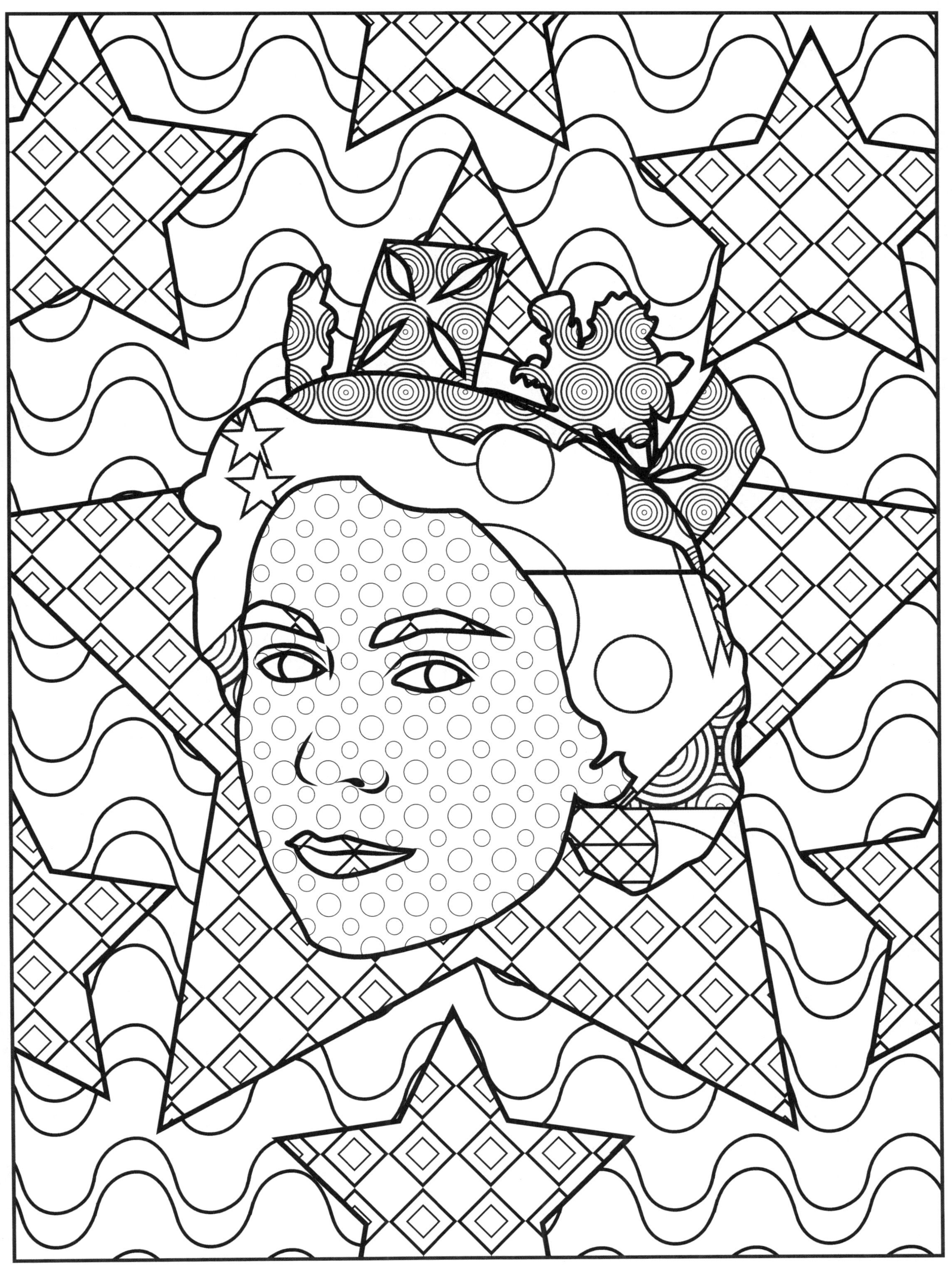

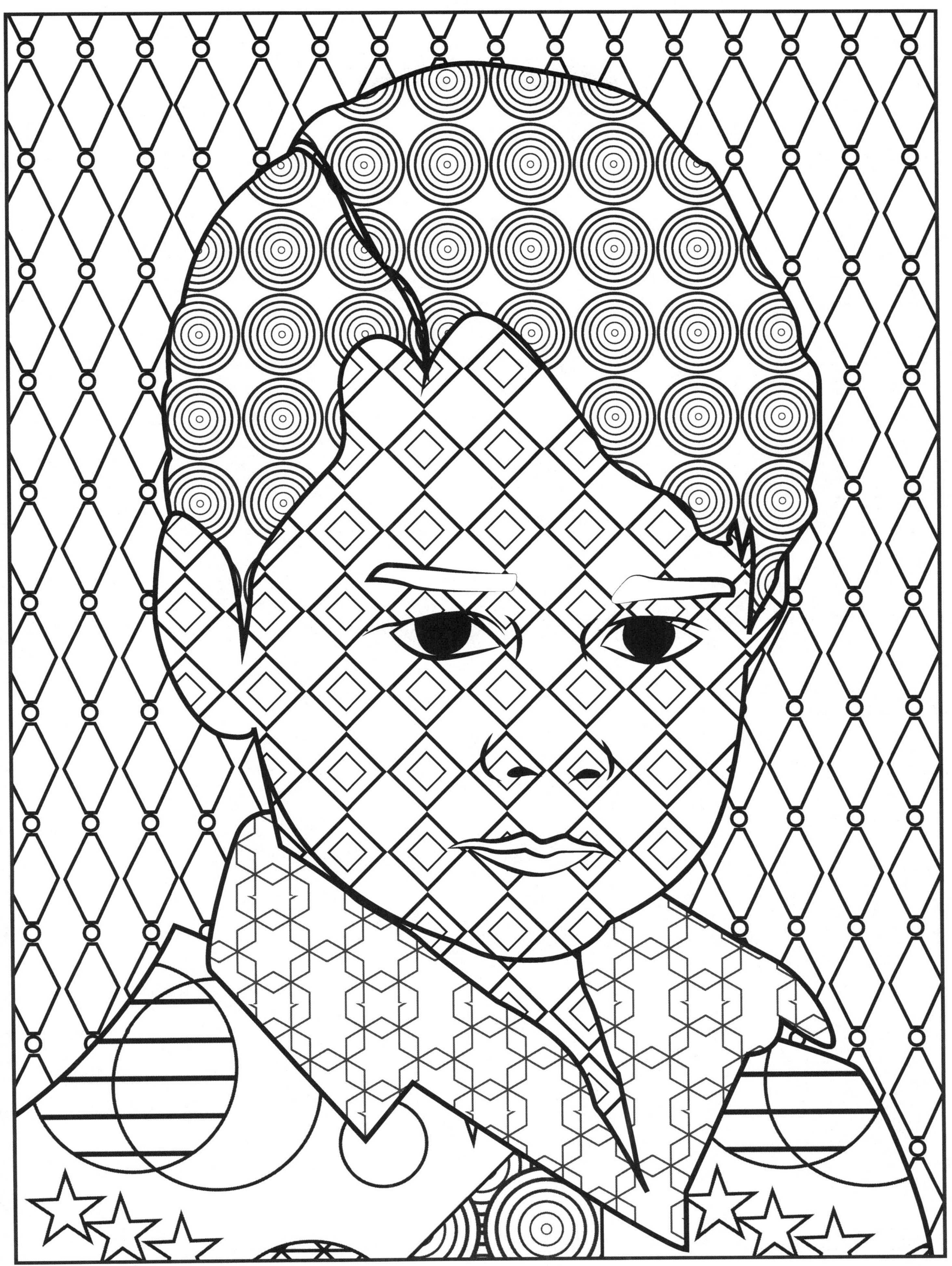

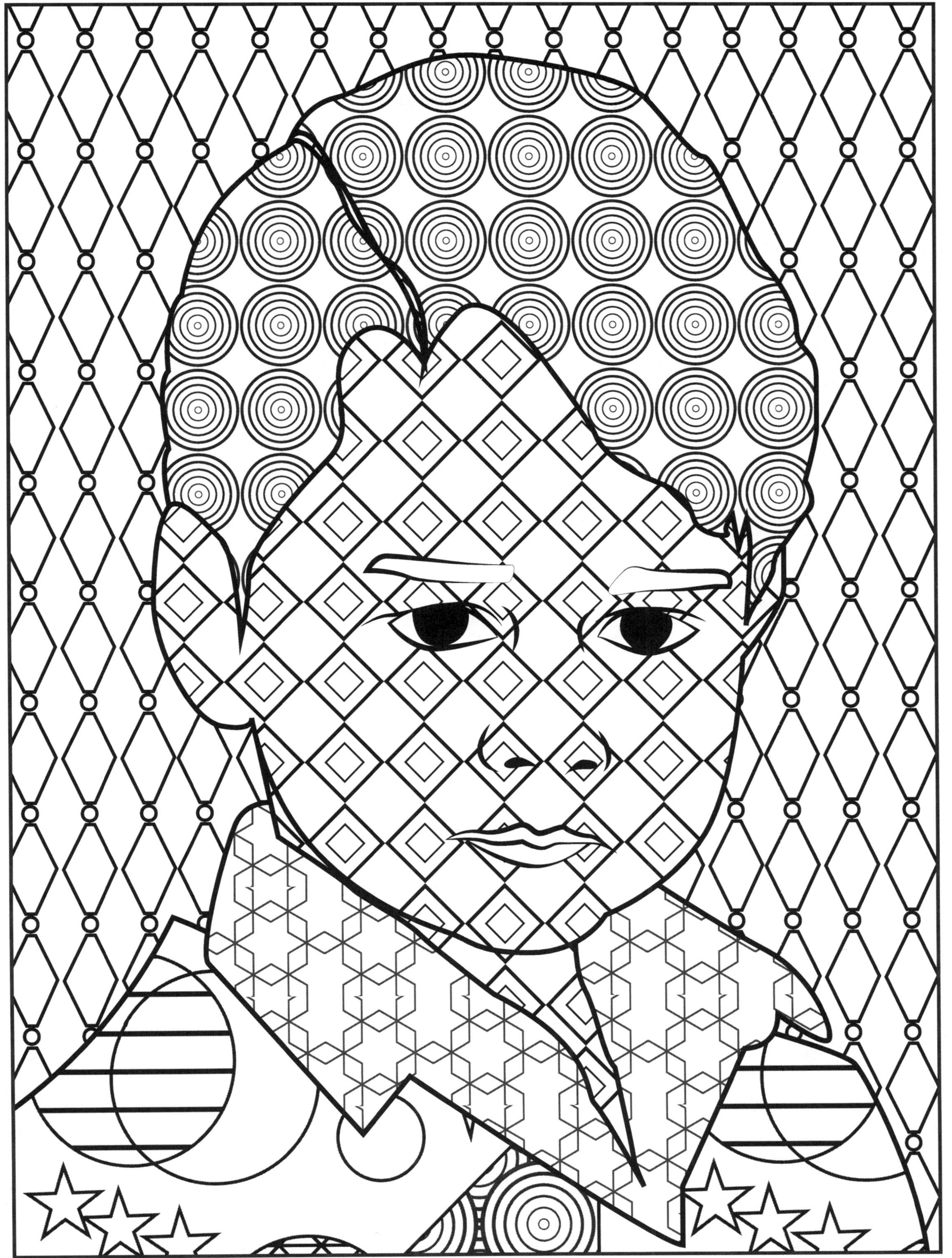

Made in the USA
Columbia, SC
17 January 2023

10551751R00038